*Raising Meat Goats for Profit
Is an enjoyable, no-nonsense tool for
new goat raisers, with important,
up-dated information for experienced
breeders as well.*

Raising Meat Goats

For Profit

By Gail B. Bowman

Written and illustrated by Gail Bowman
"North and South" articles co-authored with Annette Maze.

Cover photograph donated by
Gatwood Farms from Hattiesburg, MS

Bowman Communications Press
888-244-8948

Library of Congress Cataloging-in-Publication Data

Bowman, Gail B.
  Raising meat goats for profit.
  Includes Index
  1. Goats I. Title

ISBN 0-9670381-0-3

19.95 Manufactured in the United States of America

But ask the animals, and they will teach you,
Or the birds of the air, and they will tell you;
Or speak to the earth, and it will teach you,
Or let the fish of the sea inform you.
Which of all these does not know
That the hand of the Lord has done this?
In his hand is the life of every creature
And the breath of all mankind.

Job 12:7-10

Grateful acknowledgement is made to the following people:

❖ The International Boer Goat Association, American Kiko Goat Association, and the American and International Fainting Goat Associations for their kind and patient assistance.

❖ My husband David for his support and tireless encouragement.

❖ My children; Mike, Corinne, Robert, Travis and Shauna for believing in me.

❖ Annette Maze for her friendship and wisdom.

❖ Richard Bowman for his expertise in livestock nutrition.

❖ Wess Hallman, and Mary Wynne for their help and insight.

❖ Dr. Charles Lenkner and Dr. Tim Thompson for their input on Chapter 10.

❖ Claudia Marcus Gurn for donating the hoof drawings in Chapter 10.

❖ Nancy Coovert for allowing me to photograph her kids.

❖ The following ranches for donating photographs:
Boer Haven Farm
Caston Creek Ranch
Emma's Dream Farm
Golden Haze Farm
Hill Country Farms
Kids-R-Us Goat Farm
Lillie Hill Farms Meat Goats
Phil Sponenberg
Sabbath Day Farm
Sand Creek Boer Goats
Shep Land and Livestock
Wynneshire Farm

❖ All of the talented and hardworking authors in my Bibliography.

❖ My Lord Jesus for allowing me life.

Thank you,

Contents

What is a Meat Goat?

Much of the population of the United States and Canada manages to get through their entire lives without ever thinking very hard, if at all, about goats. I was brought up in a rural area in California. I raised a couple of sheep and some chickens for 4-H, and never gave a stray thought to goats. Why would I? Compared to cattle, goats are, historically, a rare commodity in many areas of this country. But times are changing. Goats' milk is now starting to appear in many grocery stores. Goat cheese is now available in some grocery stores, and in most specialty or "gourmet" shops.

Over 70% of the world's population eats goat meat. Now, the United States and Canada are beginning to join the rest of the world! All across this continent people are accepting the fact that goat meat (chevon) is a lean, healthy, delicious alternative to beef, lamb or pork. Now, thousands of dairy goat raisers, dairy cow breeders, and beef producers are finding out that there are not enough goats in this country, not if we butchered every one of

Picture 1: I have even heard stories of people who were sick and started feeling better after they started raising goats. *

them, to accommodate the demand for goat meat! That's right!   Not the export trade, but the growing and blossoming demand right here in the United States!

Did you know there are well over two million registered goats in the United States?   Where are they hiding? Actually, they are in most rural or semi-rural communities. Once you start looking for goats, they pop up everywhere. It's a little like buying a new car, suddenly everyone has one just like it.   Well, once you become aware of goats, you start seeing them behind every shed on your way home from work. The problem is that these are mostly dairy goats.   Dairy goats who are producing millions of gallons of milk that is being fed to calves or poured out on the ground because there are not enough

---

* This picture donated by Sand Creek Boer Goats in Shelley, Idaho

processors to make use of it. The world is screaming for goat meat, and we are stubbornly producing milk!

I'm going to assume that, if you are reading this book, you are already curious about meat goats. Somewhere along the way you have heard about this new industry, or you have owned or had experience with goats. Why are you drawn to meat goats? Well, maybe you just plain see the economic sense in raising a small, easy care, inexpensive animal for meat production. Maybe you've heard that you can graze goats on scrubland that will not support cattle (or much of anything else). Well, you're absolutely right!

And the rest of us? The ones that just like goats? I have heard story after story about people who had no intention of raising goats and now, once they've gotten started, just can't get enough of them. I have even heard stories of people who were sick and started feeling better soon after they bought their first goat. Maybe it is the intelligent and affectionate nature of goats. Maybe it's that they are so prolific. Maybe it's chemistry. I don't know. But I do know that every person who enjoys raising goats does not necessarily enjoy milking goats. There are some people out there who would tell you that you don't really want to raise goats if you don't care to milk. I mean, what else is there?

What about those cute little kids that they pop out in high multiples year after year? What if you could sell those kids for a profit? And not milk? No, no milking. Just breed your goats, kid them out, let them raise their kids, sell the kids and rebreed the moms. And make money. Meat goats do not take the time, attention or facilities that dairy goats do, and they are much more profitable than fiber goats. It has been said that you can feed 200 goats in the time it takes to milk 10. Well, I have arthritis and it takes me enough time to milk one goat that I could have fed 200! But I still want to raise goats. Meat goats are the perfect answer for people like me!

Picture 2: An eight month old Boer Doe.*

Breeds of Meat Goat

There are several types of 'meat' goats: Boer goats, Tennessee Fainting Goats, Kiko goats, and 'Spanish' goats (and some people would include Angoras). However, only three of these are true breeds with breed associations and standardized <u>meat</u> breed characteristics. These are the Boers, Kikos and Tennessee Fainting goats. The 'Spanish' goats are an indigenous goat of the southern United States. There are a couple of breeders who have done a terrific job of breeding these animals up into a very good meat animal. However, no registry or breed standards have been developed at the time of this printing. If you are going to have a meat production herd, I encourage you to investigate all of these types of goats to develop a cross breed that is comfortable for you and that is obtainable in your area. For more information about breeders of a specific breed of meat goat you can contact the American

---

* This picture by Bowman Boer Ranch in Twin Falls, Idaho

Meat Goat Association, or one of the associations for that breed. You can find their addresses and phone numbers in the Resources section of this book.

Boer Goats

Boer goats are large framed animals resembling, in many ways, the Nubian goat. The most striking difference between a Boer goat and any other type of goat you may have seen, is the size. A Boer is a large, double muscled animal developed in Southern Africa specifically for meat and hardiness. They can consistently produce more muscling in less time than any other breed of goat, and will pass this capability to their kids. Boers are vibrantly colored and relatively uniform throughout. They are easy to raise, have mild temperaments, are affectionate, require no milking, no special care, no shearing, no fancy fences, and are too big and heavy to jump on your car! What a deal!

And you know what else? When every other breed of goat is hiding in the barn to get out of the snow, the Boer goats are eating, running and playing in it! That's right! I have read multiple articles that slanderously insist that Boer goats are picky eaters and could not stand cold weather. Well, Boers were brought into this continent through Canada, and those Canadians didn't keep them in heated barns! Most Boers put on an incredible down undercoat just like a German Shepherd dog. My oldest Boer doe refuses to go into her little goat house until the temperature gets below 10 degrees F.

Boers and Boer crosses also have huge rumen capacity. The Boer goats were developed to clear land that was too difficult to be cleared by humans. They spend a lot more time grazing than other types of goats do. One reason for this, is that they are out grazing in the heat of the day when the dairy goats are wilting in the shade. They are also out grazing when the snow is blowing across the pasture. They will graze and thrive on ground that will not support dairy goats without supplementation.

Boer Goats - General Appearance.

In general appearance, Boers are usually white with a reddish brown head and (usually) a white blaze down the middle of the face. Solid red Boer goats are also becoming more and more popular. Boers have long ears that should hang down along the sides of their faces, a broad head with a convex (roman) nose and horns that curve back. The general bone structure of a Boer goat is bigger and thicker than in other breeds of goat. Since the Boer is a meat animal, the general appearance gives the viewer an impression of strength and power. Mature weights between 200 and 350 pounds for males and 120 to 200 pounds for females are considered normal!

A Short History.

Boer goats come to us from South Africa. The earliest recorded goats in Africa were brought to western Uganda by the Black Nations as early as AD 1200. Boer goats were developed in Southern Africa by breeding these 'indigenous' stock to European imports. The point, of course, was to have a hardy, very adaptable, meat animal that could survive the varied conditions of the African landscape while still maintaining a high birth rate, high survival rate, and a marketable meat carcass.

Researchers have had little luck pinning down an exact line of decent for the modern Boer goat. Early breeders include such varied and inexact groups as the "Southern Bantu" people, the Namaqua Hottentots, the Indians (from India) and Europeans. "Boer" means "farm" in Dutch.[1]

By the beginning of the 20th century, however, the breed was becoming much more distinct as the ranchers in the Eastern Cape Province of Africa started breeding for a definite meat type goat with many of the Boer characteristics that we recognize today. The late Mr T. B. Jordaan of Buffelsfontein, Somerset East, stated in the first journal of the South African Boer Goat Breeders' Association published in 1959, that his father, Mr. W. G. Jordaan, bought some goats from Mrs. Van de Venter of Somerset East. These goats were short haired and had light red heads. At the same time he bought a very large dapple-colored male goat from Mr. I. B. van Heerden of Kaalplass, Cradock. From these goats, some of the earliest breeding stock was developed.[2]

On July 4th, 1959, breeding and selection became regulated by the foundation of the Boer Goat Breeder's Association (of South Africa). In the past forty years, the breed standards of this association have helped to guide and mold the Boer goat into an "improved" breed emphasizing good overall conformation, a compact and well muscled body structure, high growth and fertility rates, short white hair, darkly pigmented skin, and red markings on the head and shoulders. In 1970 the Boer goat was incorporated into the National Mutton Sheep and Goat Performance Testing Scheme, which makes the Boer goat the only known goat breed involved in a performance test for meat production.[3]

In 1977, the Boer goat was imported into Germany. In 1987 Lancorp Corporation Ltd. imported Boers into New Zealand, and in 1988 they were imported into Australia. The first Boer embryos to reach the North American Continent were implanted into recipient does at Olds College in Canada. These goats stayed in quarantine until April 1993, when Boers were released into the United States and Canada. In New Zealand, three main parties were involved in the importation of South African Boer Goats: Lancorp Corporation Ltd., Embryotech Corporation, and African Goat Flock Co. In Australia the major importer was Australian Breeding Management Pty Ltd. [2]

Since 1987 the Boer goat has been imported by New Zealand, Canada, Germany, Mexico, Australia, Indonesia, England, India, France, Malaysia, Denmark, British West Indies, Netherland Antilles, and virtually every state in the United States.

Breed Standards:

The breed standards of the International Boer Goat Association are the most recently compiled set of standards at the time of this printing. In the main, I have quoted them as they were written. However, in the discussion of defects, I have paraphrased for the purposes of this book. (Breed standards are also available from the American, South African, Canadian, Australian and New Zealand Boer Goat Associations.) A lot of the terminology in this section is very technical. For those who find it difficult to follow, I have provided a simple diagram of goat physiology at the end of this chapter.

International Boer Goat Association
South African Boer Goat Breed Standards

General Appearance
The Boer goat is a meat animal and as such the general appearance should give an impression of size and strength. The bucks should be substantially larger than does with a broad chest, a strong back and double muscled rump. Their head should be broad with a convex nose and horns that curve back. Does should also appear broad with a firm stance, meaty chest and strong rump and thighs; but with a more feminine appearance. The overall appearance should be that of a strong, well built meat producer.

Head Shape and Color
The Boer goat should have a strong head with brown eyes. A desirable head should have a smooth and continuous convex curve from the nose to the apex of the horn. Horns should be round, darkly colored, and moderately to widely spaced. Does may have their horns removed with no discrimination shown against them. Ears are to be flat and hang smoothly along the side of the face, avoiding the eyes. The bottom tip of the ear may be folded. The jaws must fit well.

A totally red head, or a red head with a white blaze or white spot is ideal. The red should range in shade from light to dark red, although orange, brown or reddish black will be accepted. The minimum color requirement for breeding stock should be a patch of red at least 40% on both sides of the head, excluding the ears. Both ears should have at least 75% red coloring to be ideal, however

50% is acceptable as long as there is at least 75% overall pigmentation of the head area.

Defects of the head include horns that are too straight or too flat, pointed or pinched jaws, protruding ears or ears that are too short, lack of color on the head, folded ears involving the ear canal, concave foreheads, undershot or overshot jaws, blue eyes, and a crooked face.

Front End Assembly
In bucks, the neck should be well fleshed and of moderate length in proportion to the length of the body. Does should have a more feminine extension of the neck. The breastbone should be wide and deep into the brisket. The shoulder should be wide and smooth across the top to demonstrate volume and rest flush against the withers. The front end assembly should be of sufficient height to be slightly elevated over the back.

Defects of the front end assembly include loose, winged or open shoulders, narrow chest or pinched heartgirth, a neck that is too narrow or short, a "U" shaped neck, a protruding breastbone.

Back
The back should be broad and long. A slight dip behind withers is permissible to allow rotation. The wide loin should be long and well covered. The rump should be long and slightly level. Hindquarters should have good extension to fully fleshed thighs. Thigh should be round, well muscled and extend far down the back leg. Pinbones should be wide and well placed. The tail must be straight where it grows out of the dock and swing to either side.

Defects of the back include the back being too concave, the loin too narrow or short or lacking covering, the back lacking length throughout, a wry or broken tail, pinbones that are too narrow, a sway back, a steep rump, too long in the shank, flat hindquarters or rump.

Legs, Pasterns & Feet
Front legs should be straight and long enough to give sufficient height to front end assembly. Front legs should be placed in correct proportion to the front end, and

directly under the withers. Front pasterns should be short and straight. Front and rear hooves should be black and have tight toes that are pointing directly forward. Back legs should be set wide apart and straight when viewed from the rear with clean hocks. A good balance between bone refinement and strength is essential. The rear legs should be nearly perpendicular from hocks to pasterns when viewed from the side. Rear pasterns should be short to medium length. Feet should be strong with tight toes pointed directly forward with deep heels and the sole nearly uniform in depth from heel to toe. Animal should track with sufficient width between legs both fore and rear.

Defects of the feet and legs include knees that are too close, enlarged knees, legs that are too fleshy or too thin, weak pasterns, crooked feet, hind legs too close together, sprung pasterns, or bowed over knees.

Skin and Coverings
A loose and supple skin with sufficient chest and neck folds, especially on the bucks, is essential. Eyelids and hairless parts must be pigmented. The hairless skin under the tail should have 75% pigmentation for stud purposes with 100% pigmentation the ideal.

The body should ideally be white, but 20% spotting or coloration is permitted. Solid colors, other than white, will not be discriminated against. Short glossy hair is desirable showing freedom from coarseness. A limited amount of winter down will be tolerated during winter months.

Defects of the skin and coverings include skin that is too tight, coarse hair, hair that is too long, a tail that is less than 75% pigmented, pink eyelids, pink tail, skin that is too lightly pigmented.

Reproductive Organs
The does should have a well-formed mammary system. It should consist of good attachments and no more than two separated functional teats per side of udder. A functional teat has an orifice in it. Ideally, does should have one teat

per udder half. The bucks should have two large, well formed equal sized testes in a single scrotum. The apex of the scrotum may have a split no longer than 1 inch (2.5 cm). Scrotal circumference varies with the age of the buck. The normal circumference is 10 inches (25.5 cm) on a yearling buck and 12 inches (30.5 cm) on a two year old buck. Teat structure on the male should consist of no more than two separated teats per side. Ideally, bucks should have one teat per side.

Defects of the reproductive organs include testicles that twist while the buck walks, more than 2 teats per side, small or abnormal testicles, scrotal split of more than 1 inch, a split teat with two distinctly separate milk ducts, bunched or clustered teats.[4]

Kiko Goats

The Kiko goat is a recent development of a New Zealand company called "Goatex Group LLC". These hardy goats were developed as a result of a government funded project to get the native goat population in New Zealand under control. As part of this project, in the 1970's, many goats were hunted and killed, and thousands more were captured to cross with angoras.

Some of the native goats confined during this project exhibited enhanced characteristics for growth and meat production. The members of Goatex isolated these animals and began to cross them with hair and milk goats to find a combination that would yield the best results in both hardiness and meat carcass production. The resulting breed was called "Kiko" meaning "meat for consumption" in Maori.

The Kiko goat registry was established in 1991 in New Zealand. The characteristics that have been carefully defined and bred for have more to do with incredible hardiness, breeding abilities and meat production, than with appearance. Kikos began to be introduced to the United States in 1994. In addition, the Kiko goat registry

Picture 3: A Boer buck.**

Picture 4: A Kiko buck.*

** This picture by Bowman Boer Ranch in Twin Falls, Idaho.
* This picture donated by Caston Creek Ranch from Wister, Oklahoma

maintains a registry for Kiko/Boer crosses called "Genemasters".[5]

Breed Standards:

In the main, I have quoted the breed standards as they were written. However, in the discussion of defects, I have paraphrased for the purposes of this book.

Kiko Goat Registry - North America
Kiko Goat Breed Standard

The Kiko Goat is bred and raised as a meat producer and the breed standard recognizes the relationship between the physical characteristics of the animal and its production capabilities.

General Characteristics
The primary characteristic of the Kiko goat is its hardiness and its ability to achieve substantial weight gains when run under natural conditions without supplementary feeding. In addition, the female is capable of conceiving, carrying, giving birth to and rearing multiple offspring without intervention under less than ideal conditions. The Kiko is an aggressive forager capable of thriving under conditions of feed deprivation and any characteristic which detracts from its ability to range and forage should be severely penalized.

Head
A strong head with bold expression. A moderate forehead lets into a well proportioned nose, neither convex nor concave. Nostrils wide with a slight flare. Eyes generally brown with alert expression. Eye color other than brown should not be penalized. Mouth well formed with tight lips over well fitting jaws: slight undershot permissible as an aid in browsing. Horns well spaced, strong and solid with a characteristic outward sweep. Mature males display a distinctive shallow spiral in horn growth. Horns may be cropped in animals greater than twelve months of age without penalty. Ears comparatively high set and of medium breath and moderate length, not pendulous. Prick ears are undesirable.

Characteristic culling faults of the head include concave or convex face, a roman nose, an overshot jaw, an excessively undershot jaw, horns that are swept back or too close together, toughing the neck, or too straight or parrot mouth.

Neck and Forequarter
Neck medium in length and well proportioned relative to body capacity: full and well muscled and flowing into forequarter. Shoulder well laid and well muscled with tight attachment. Forechest prominent and strong but in proportion to body size. Front legs strong with good shoulder angulation - length from wither to elbow should approximate length from elbow to ground. Pasterns strong with well formed hooves.

Characteristic culling faults of the neck and forequarter include a neck that is too long or too thin, bull neck, loose shoulders.

Body
Body long, broad and compact. Ribs well sprung and of moderate length displaying good girth. Loins long and well fleshed. Back strong and reasonably straight.

Characteristic culling faults of the body include excessively short back or slab sides.

Hindquarters
Rump broad and flat without severe slope. Thighs well fleshed to the hock. Hocks well angulated. Tail straight and mobile.

Characteristic culling faults of the hindquarters include a rump that is steep or short, straight hocks, or poorly fleshed thighs.

Legs and feet
Strong and well placed indicating endurance and agility. Legs should be parallel, well angulated and turn neither in nor out. Strong hocks and pasterns. Hooves neatly formed with pronounced interdigital division. Any condition of the hoof which affects the animal's ability to move freely should be severely penalized.

Characteristic culling faults of the legs and feet include forelegs that turn in or out, cowhocks or sickle hocks, poor rear angulation, dropped pasterns, or any abnormality of the hoof.

Skin and coat
Smooth supple skin which is neither tight nor loose. Some dewlap may be evident in mature males and should not be penalized. Skin may be pigmented or not, but darker skin is to be preferred. The coat may vary according to climatic conditions and there is a marked variation between summer and winter coats. Coat may vary from short, slick and lustrous to moderately profuse hair: the former is to be preferred but the later should not be penalized. Some down appearing in the coat is permissible. Wattles occasionally appear and should not be penalized. The predominant color is white which is desirable but any other color is equally permissible.

Reproductive organs
Males: testicles even sized and well formed.   Scrotum undivided, compact and held high.   Sheath neat and accessible.
Females: udder well formed, moderately capacious and well attached.   Two well placed, medium sized, functional teats   with   adequate   orifices.   Non-functional supernumerary teats should not be penalized.

Characteristic culling faults of the reproductive organs include, in males, divided scrotum, small testicles, pendulous scrotum or a loose sheath. For females, a split udder, pendulous udder, more than two functional teats, or poor udder attachment. Also hermaphroditism.

Size and appearance
A medium to large animal displaying the ability to produce meat. Mature animals tend to be square with the height of the animal from the wither to the ground approximating its length from the wither to the root of the tail. The forechest should reach to the elbow of the foreleg. Males are distinctively larger than females and each sex unmistakably displays the characteristics of its gender.

Characteristic culling faults of size and appearance include excessive leg length, insufficient size, masculine females and feminine males.[6]

Tennessee Fainting Goats

The Tennessee Fainting Goat has been traced back to Marshall County, Tennessee in the 1880's. The story is, that a man named Tinsley drifted into town bringing with him a few goats. When he left, he sold his goats to a man named R. Goode, who was fascinated by these unusual goats. There is no recorded history of these goats before that time.[7] Since then, fainting goats have been used mainly for meat, but also to protect sheep. They say that if you have a fainting goat in your herd, and coyotes or dogs attack the herd, the sheep will run away but the fainting goat will fall over allowing the predator an easy meal while the sheep escape! Handy for the sheep, but not too fun for the goats.

The name 'fainting' goat is actually a misnomer. The goats don't actually faint. They have a genetic characteristic which causes their muscles to stiffen up on them. Whenever they are startled or surprised their muscles lock up and they sometimes fall over. These goats have about 40% more muscle than the average dairy goat of the same size. They are also called 'Nervous' goats and 'Stiff-legged' goats.

Fainting goats are not huge animals. They average between 17 and 25 inches tall, and weigh between 50 and 165 pounds. They come in a wide variety of coats and colors, with long ears that stand out to the sides of their heads. Fainting goats have very distinctive 'bulgy' eyes. Several breeders have spent a lot of time and energy breeding this basic breed up into an 'improved' meat goat that is larger and heavier and crosses well with Boers.

Picture 5: A Tennessee Fainting Goat buck.*

Breed Standards:

In the main, I have quoted the breed standards as they were written.

International Fainting Goat Breed Standard

General Appearance
The Fainting Goat is of small-medium size. Its frame is well defined and clearly angulated. Its limbs are somewhat shorter than its body length. The body is full barreled with muscling throughout. The height and weight circumference is greater than in full size goats, but not as great as in the pygmy goat. The fainting goat is usually a somewhat shy, though alert, good-natured animal.

---

* This picture donated by Sabbath Day Farm from Linneus, Maine.

Breed Characteristics:

Coat
The full coat of straight to wavy hair, medium in length, varies in density with the seasons and climates. On females, beards may be non-existent or sparse, or trimmed; on adult males, abundant hair growth is desirable but not mandatory; the beard to be full, with good length, the mane to also have good length to drape across the shoulders.

Color
All colors are acceptable, with the exception of a solid grey or silver goat which is the least desirable. The predominant coloration is black and white with any denomination thereof. All shades of brown or brown and white.

Markings
Any markings are acceptable with the exception of that of other breeds of goats.

Head
The head should be short to medium long, profile fairly straight. Muzzle should be slightly rounded; not snipey; nose medium in length, wide and flat. Chin and underjaw full; bite even, neither over nor undershot; jaws fairly broad and flat. Eyes not set too close together, prominent, even slightly protruding. Ears medium in size, mostly erect, somewhat tilted forward, while being alert and mobile. Genetically horned or polled goats are acceptable.

Neck
The neck should be well muscled; of medium length, with a slightly rounder more full throated appearance than that of full size goats; more slender in females than in males.

Shoulder
The shoulders should be somewhat muscular, well angulated and well laid on; point of shoulder placed posterior to prosternum.

Back
The back should be strong; almost level along chine and loin; rising slightly toward the iliac crest.

Loin
The loin should be nearly level, strong with good width.

Mammary System
Udder
The udder should be firm and rounded, medium to large in size. The rear attachment to be symmetrical, high, halves evenly balanced. The front attachment to be well forward and attached, without pocket, blending smoothly into the body. The texture to be free of lumps or scar tissue, pliable but firm, very smooth. The teats to be of uniform size and length, cylindrical, free of obstructions, deformities, or multiple orifices. Placed symmetrically on the udder.

Reproductive System in Bucks
The testicles should be two fully descended, and of equal size, showing firmness. The teats to be two, symmetrical and non-functional.[8]

Conclusion

Many people ask me which breed of goat they should buy to start their meat herd. My answer is always the same: "What do you want to do with your goats?" What breed of goat you raise depends on where you live, what you like, what you are going to feed, and what is available to you in your area. There does seem to be one factor that is common to most meat producers that I have spoken to, whether they are raising Kiko, Spanish, Fainting, Angora or dairy, or a mixture of all of the above. They all seem to cross their goats with Boers. I have to assume that this is because the Boers are the older breed, they are very large, and they tend to throw consistent amounts of meat. So, again, my advice is: "Shop around. Find out what you like, *really* like what you like; go buy it, and then have fun raising it!"

Goat Anatomy

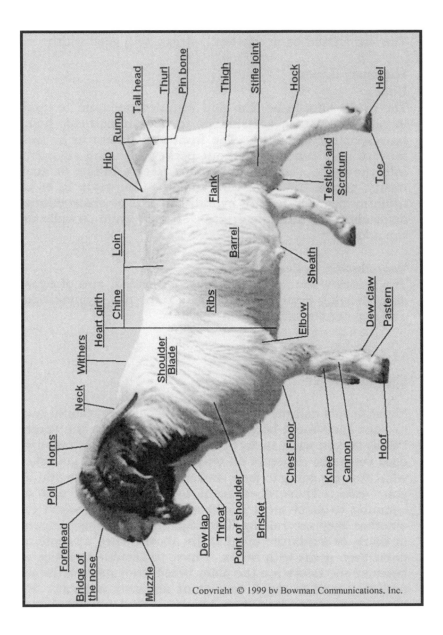

Copyright © 1999 by Bowman Communications, Inc.

Why Raise Meat Goats?

Studies show that the goat meat industry is the fastest growing livestock industry in the United States. The main reason is that the goat meat industry is not looking for someone who is willing to try an unknown meat for the novelty of it, as the buffalo and ostrich breeders have been. Meat goat producers are not raising an 'exotic' product. Goat meat is already eaten by 70% of the population of the world, and it has been since the beginning of time. What we *are* breeding is a better, bigger, meatier animal. Goat meat is seeking market acceptance in the western culture, and is offering an alternative to some of the failing agricultural products in the United States, and the world.

The demand for 'chevon', or 'cabrito', or 'goat meat' in the United States is so high that producers can't keep up. Because of this vacuum, much of the goat meat sold in the United States is imported from New Zealand or Australia. About 1.5 million pounds of goat meat is imported every week.[9] And demand just keeps growing.

Much of the demand is generated by the changing ethnic demographics of the continent. About 63% of the red meat consumed worldwide is goat! Much of the goat meat demand in the United States comes from ethnic groups that include Middle Eastern, Asian, African, Latin American and Caribbean heritage. Most of these groups buy goat meat whenever they can find it, and they are willing to pay better prices for higher quality meat.

One of the things that we, as producers, need to focus on is educating non-ethnic consumers about the palatability of this fantastic product.

Chevon

What is so special about chevon (goat meat)? Many people have digestive problems that require a careful diet. The molecular structure of chevon is different than that of other meats. Therefore, chevon digests more easily. It is also a low fat, good tasting alternative to chicken or fish. Here is a table that shows the comparative nutrition of chevon:[10]

3 oz roasted	Calories	Fat (g)	Sat. Fat (g)	Protein (g)	Iron (g)
Chevon	122	2.58	.79	23	3.2
Chicken	120	3.5	1.1	21	1.5
Beef	245	16.0	6.8	23	2.0
Pork	310	24.0	8.7	21	2.7
Lamb	235	16.0	7.3	22	1.4

I am one of those people who have to watch what they eat. I can eat chicken, some kinds of fish, turkey and chevon. I prefer chevon from an animal that is at least 75% Boer. The Boer influence changes the taste of the meat to a milder, more veal-like flavor. When you have as few choices in your diet as I do, you learn what you like. I have not had the opportunity to try Kiko or Fainting goat meat. My comparisons are with dairy goat meat.

The Direct Market Niche

In our area, if you put out the word that you have meat goats for sale, you usually have enough calls to sell your animals right off your ranch. I get about $1.00 per pound on the hoof. I have had other breeders tell me that they can get more for goats with Boer blood. This is a good example of one way to market your goats – find a profitable direct market niche.

One of the most popular market niches in the meat goat industry today is the direct market. A 'direct market' is a group or type of buyer that will come directly to your ranch to buy from you, for a specific reason. There are many direct market niches for meat goats.[11]

I have already suggested one type of direct market niche: the ethnic meat market. In most communities in the United States today, there are people who highly value goat meat, especially in the spring. If you can identify a means of reaching this group, you can sell directly from your ranch because they know that you are raising good, healthy animals.

Another direct market niche involves the growing trend in the 4-H and FFA clubs to raise meat goats. 4-H and FFA youth will usually pay a higher price for your best wethers, for show wethers, than you would have received if you had sold them by the pound.

One of the most profitable direct market niches supplies Chevon to the local restaurants that are serving an ethnic clientele. Many breeders find that they can tap into this niche by offering the restaurant owners a 'sample' of the product.

Another direct market niche is the market for meat breeding stock. Commercial meat breeders will usually pay about double, for breeding stock, what you might have expected to receive for the same animal by the pound. However, to tap into this market you will have to have stock that is worth buying for breeding. Not necessarily fullblood anything, but at least part meat goat, and in good condition.

A direct market niche that does not occur to a lot of people is the sale of goats to hobbyists. One such hobby is pack goating. Many people in my area are buying goat kids at 4 days to 4 weeks old to train to be pack goats. These people castrate the bucks, and 'humanize' them so that they will stay with them on a hiking trip. They then teach the goats to carry specially made packs. Many 'packers' buy meat cross kids because they have more muscle than dairy goats, so they can carry more weight. This may seem silly to you, but meat breeders in my area have been selling several buck kids per year at only 4 days old. This works well if you have a doe who has had triplets, for instance. Packers pay between $50 and $125 per kid for pack goats.

The Commercial Meat Market

Many breeders are now working together, in cooperatives or associations, to meet large commercial sales contracts. These contracts supply the meat markets on the east and west coasts of the United States, and require a supply of high numbers of animals, of a consistent quality, on a regular basis. At this time, much of the meat for these contracts is being imported because there just are not enough meat goats in the United States to supply the contracts.

However, as production expands, more and more of these contracts will be met locally. If there is a meat co-op or association in your area, I would suggest that you get 'plugged in' and do everything you can to help them get started.

In many areas of the country, slaughter houses are being constructed specifically for goat meat. However, almost none of the goats being processed at these facilities are actually meat type goats. There are just not enough meat goats being raised, which are not pre-sold to direct markets, to supply a production facility.

Fullblood Breeding Stock

Fullblood breeding animals are a whole different industry from the meat production industry. However, the two are very closely tied. When you take a look at what you want to raise, you might consider adding at least a few quality fullbloods to your operation. If the meat industry in your area blooms and expands, there will be more demand for good fullblood meat goats. I think that the market for poor, low producing fullblood stock has already gone by the wayside. We are heading into an era of serious meat production.

In all livestock industries, there is a place for the good registered herd sire. These animals must be proven to be fertile and prolific, adaptable, disease free, and have the meat and muscle characteristics that will add productivity to a commercial meat herd. As we discuss the profitability of raising meat goats, consider whether or not you want to make the initial investment to start a good breeding stock herd. Or, alternatively, add a few breeding stock to your meat herd, or some meat production stock to your fullblood herd.

The two types are not mutually exclusive. As a matter of fact, one usually leads to the other. If you start with a meat herd, but have to add a fullblood herd sire, sometimes you will also be tempted to buy a fullblood doe to go with him. Then you are suddenly producing herd sires for your neighbors. This is a good idea, because one good fullblood sale a year can pay nearly 1/5th of your feed costs for a year (if you are raising 50 goats).

On the other hand, if you are raising fullbloods, do you have a large enough fullblood market to sell everything you will be producing? Would it be a better idea to raise a herd made up of half fullbloods, and the other half some type of cross breeds? Dairy goats, angora goats or Spanish goats crossed with a fullblood meat animal, and sold for breeding stock to meat herds, will bring more income per head than a meat animal sold by the pound. Of course, you will still end up with some extra wethers, there is no avoiding it, but these are your meat products, to be sold by the pound. You have still sold the majority of your kids for a direct market price, and made a good profit.

What are the prices on fullblood meat goats expected to be in the long run? Many things will affect the answer to that question. I know a couple who breed fullblood registered angus cattle. How many rural communities have plenty of cattle? How can these people make their money? They market. They have big production sales where breeders come from all over the world, or tie into a satellite link, to buy their stock. I believe that there will always be top breeding stock. People that advertise, raise quality disease free animals, and let the meat producers know they are out there, will always have a market.

The price you will be able to get will depend on the quality of your animals and the effectiveness of your advertising. If you do not want to market, you will probably be able to sell your fullbloods to your neighbors at about $250, indefinitely. If you are well known, and advertise (we will talk about marketing strategies in Chapter 9), and you have animals that make the buyer's head turn, you will probably always be able to get at least $800 for your fullblood meat goats. At the time of this printing the prices for good fullblood stock are about double that amount, and are actually going up. These prices have been stable for three years now, so I am betting that they will remain firm in the future. All livestock, or agricultural, businesses are a gamble, though. We will just have to wait and see.

Meat Production for Profit

There are many issues to consider when you are deciding to raise livestock for a profit. First of all, you must find out if you are going to have an economical way to feed your animals. The most economical way to feed ruminant animals is, of course, the pasture. However, to put the weight onto your meat animals that will be necessary to get top dollar on sale day, you must have very good pasture. Even with superb pasture you should consider that you will probably need to creep feed your kids to get them to market weight at an early age. So you need to look into reasonably priced creep feeds that will add protein and energy to your kid's diet in a compact package. In other words, pelletized mixed-grain products intended for young ruminants.

If you will be feeding hay, you need to consider what kind of hay is available in your area that would be suitable for your meat animals. The best feed program may be a combination of feeds. For instance, an alfalfa pellet will supply good calcium, energy and protein, and can be used in combination with a less nutritious, inexpensive hay product.

The following is a 4 year projected ledger for a meat goat production ranch, per six goats (studies show you can raise about 6 goats or 1 cow per 1 acre of good pasture). I have assumed that you have 7 months of graze, and will have to feed for 5 months. I have also assumed that you have more animals than this, so all the costs (like breeding fees) will be percentages of an greater whole. I have included a parallel projection for a cow.

Month	Per 6 Goat	Costs	Sales	Per Cow	Costs	Sales
Year 1						
July	Buy 6 does	$900		Buy a cow	$450	
August	Buy feed for winter/ hay	$225		Buy feed for winter/ hay	$150	
September	Buy/rent a buck - breed	$180		Buy/rent a bull - breed	$60	
October						
November						
December						
January						
February	Goats kid with 1.5 kids					
March						
April						
May	3 of the goats rebreed					
June				Cow calves with 1 calf		

Month	Per 6 Goat	Costs	Sales	Per Cow	Costs	Sales
Year 2						
July	Buy feed for winter/ hay	$225		Buy feed for winter/ hay	$150	
August	Sell 9 kids $75		$675			
September	Breed other 3 goats			breed		
September	3 Goats kid with 1.5 kids					
October						
November						
December	Rebreed the 3 Sept goats			Sell calf		$350
January						
February	3 Goats kid with 1.5 kids					
March	Sell 4.5 kids $75		$337			
April						
May	3 Goats kid with 1.5 kids					
June				Cow calves with 1 calf		
Year 3						
July	Buy feed for winter/ hay	$225		Buy feed for winter/ hay	$150	
August	Sell 4.5 kids $75		$337			
September	Breed all 6 goats			Breed		
October	Sell 4.5 kids $75		$337			
November						
December				Sell calf		$350
January						
February	6 Goats kid with 1.5 kids					
March						
April						
May	Rebreed 3 of the goats					
June				Cow calves with 1 calf		

Month	Per 6 Goat	Costs	Sales	Per Cow	Costs	Sales
Year 4						
July	Buy feed for winter/ hay	$225		Buy feed for winter/ hay	$150	
August	Sell 9 kids $75		$675			
September	Breed 3 goats			breed		
October	3 Goats kid with 1.5 kids					
November						
December				Sell calf		$350
January	Rebreed the 3 Oct goats					
February	3 Goats kid with 1.5 kids					
March						
April	Sell 4.5 kids $75		$337			
May						
June	3 Goats kid with 1.5 kids			Cow calves with 1 calf		
Total		**$1980**	**$2698**		**$1110**	**$1050**
Unsold assets	6 kids		$675	1 calf		$350
Total		$1980	$3373		$1110	$1400
Profit			**$1393**			**$300**
Profit X 50 (300 goats)		**$69,650**		**Profit X 50 (50 cows)**		**$15,000**

There are a lot of variables that would affect the above table. I have assumed that three, and only three, of your goats are rebreeding on a short schedule. I have assumed that 1.5 of the kids born to each doe (not the more typical 2.0), and every calf born, survive to go to market. I have not taken into account standard expenses that go into running a ranch: Hired labor, vet fees, vaccinations and wormers, repairs, vehicles, taxes, etc. However, I have also not taken into account the possibility that you might get more than $75 for some of your kids in a direct market niche.

As you can see, a meat herd requires a good manager. Most of us can barter for many of the products and labor we need. I have also allowed $150 per doe for meat production does (dairy, Spanish, or some cross). I have allowed this amount because, if you are going to keep expenses down, you cannot buy your base stock from the auction yards. You will save enough money in vet fees and fatalities, by buying healthy animals from a breeder, to make up the difference in the original price of the doe in the first year.

We all cut corners when we are trying to make a profit, but don't cut yourself out of business. You can buy fullblood or cross bred meat goats for a lower price if the goat has some flaw or disease. Shop for the flaws that do not matter to your meat operation (see the discussion on flaws in the chapter on breeding), *but stay well away from the diseases*. You might save money by replacing the engine in your old truck instead of buying a new one, but don't skimp on your worming and vaccination schedule. Shop for the best feed prices you can find, but take the time to evaluate what is in your feeds so you are not throwing away your money on feed that is nutritionally unsound.

Combining Goats with Other Livestock

Goats can be a good companion livestock with cattle or sheep if they are in conditions where they can browse. If given a choice, goats will eat brush and tall weeds, cattle eat tall grass, and sheep eat shorter grasses. Goats and sheep tend to graze the high ground, while cattle prefer to stay in the valleys. Grazing a combination of these different livestock can help you to manage risk, and promote plant diversity on our rangelands.

Researchers at the U.S. Sheep Experiment Station in Dubois, Idaho, found they could increase rangeland stocking rates by 60% when they grazed cattle and sheep together. They also found that plant species diversity increased.[12] Although these studies do not include goats, you can see that the parallel would apply.

There are advantages, and disadvantages, to combining species on rangeland. For one thing, chevon prices are on the rise, while beef prices have dropped. Different species also have their young at different times of the year. This can insure that you have production stock to sell more often during the year. However, some ranchers worry that they would need to keep the cattle away from the goats when they are kidding. However, goats' natural instincts would cause them to go and find a hollow or bush to kid in, so it is unlikely that they would be bothered by the cattle.

If you are already set up for cattle, you may find that raising goats will bring you new challenges and opportunities. You cannot treat a goat in a cattle squeeze chute, if that is what you already have. On the other hand, you can't treat a cow by running her into a corral and catching her, either. If you come across a goat that is having trouble kidding, you don't need any special equipment to help her out. The vaccines that are used for cattle are generally used for goats, too. And if your bucks run the range with the does, you will automatically be kidding year-around, maximizing your profit potential.

Both sheep and goats eat many weeds, including one called 'leafy spurge'. This weed costs $250 per acre to kill with chemicals. However, you can graze sheep or goats with your cattle and the weed is controlled naturally.[12] The same is true of many other types of weeds, including thistles, Russian olive trees and berry bushes.

With the economic climate changing in the agricultural industries, we all need to be looking for ways to maximize our profit potential, while fully utilizing our resources. Goats kid in high multiples, on a relatively short cycle. Meat goats are low maintenance, and can thrive in relatively poor conditions. Soon, we will see cattle and goats grazing together in more areas, just because it makes good economic sense.

NOTES:

3

Getting Started with Facilities

Having 'facilities' means having an appropriate place to put your goats once you get them home. So many times we buy our animals without really giving enough thought to what we are going to do with them when they get off the truck. Goats, however, are not the type of animal that will stay where you put them without some planning on your part.

Beginning facilities for a goat ranch must include good fencing, some reasonable housing, waterers, feeders, a place to store feeds, and possibly, a guard animal. I know this sounds like a lot, but it really isn't as bad as it sounds, and will be a lot easier if you plan to take care of it before the goats get home to help.

Fencing for Goats

Fencing is an unwelcome expense that every goat raiser must bear. Like so many others, I was unwilling to spend much money on fencing when we started raising goats.

We put up 33 foot X 100 foot pens out of four foot welded wire on steel posts that were about 12 foot apart.   It lasted one year. The strands of the welded wire would not hold up to the goats because they rubbed on it and stood on it to look over.   The strands literally broke apart, causing a strangulation hazard. We started again, this time learning to do it right.

Any breeder of dairy or pygmy goats can tell you horror stories about trying to keep their animals in fences. I have never had trouble with goats jumping my fences, because I have always raised meat goats, and meat goats are generally a calmer crowd.   Meat goats are also heavier than most other types of goat, so they don't leap through the air as gracefully, or at all. I have heard that if you are going to use Spanish goats for your cross breeds, you need very high fences - they seem to be part antelope.

However, I am well aware that the minute I tell you that meat goats don't jump, you are going to build 3 foot fences and go buy an entire herd of high vaulters. So I am not going to do that. Goats will be goats. The only difference with meat animals is that some will jump less than others, instead of all jumping higher than the last.   Four foot fences have worked for me.   These do need to be of a dense structure, because *all goats will go through a fence* if the opportunity arises.

To make a good fence, you need four or five foot woven wire, not welded.   The type that has 2 inch by 4 inch spaces between the strands, rather than 4 inch by 6 inch spaces, is better.   The reason for the smaller holes is simply that most meat goats have horns, and they cannot get their head into a 2" by 4" hole to get their horns stuck. The fence posts should be no farther apart than 8 feet. Your fence will last a lot longer if you carry a couple bags of quick set cement and some water out to the fence line, and cement in your 4 to 6 inch treated wooden (or pipe) corner posts. Many people install a strand of electric wire on the inside of their fences, at about shoulder height to a goat (about 24 inches off the ground), and again at the top of the fence, to keep the goats from rubbing or standing on the wire.

Meat goats do better if they are not in small pens. As I said, we started with 33 by 100 foot pens, and put about 6 goats into a pen. This ratio works well if you are going to feed them a full ration. There is not enough space however, to allow for any grazing. Most people just automatically think of goats as living in pens, because that is usually the way dairy goat breeders keep goats. Let's think about this a minute. Dairy goat breeders keep their goats in pens because they need to give them a more complete feed ration to keep them producing milk, and they need to milk them twice a day. Do you have land that could be grazed? Are you going to be milking? Could your goats live outside of pens? Then why are you going to build pens?

It took me years to learn that my goats were better off living out on our 20 acre pasture than in pens. Fencing is an issue, that's true. However, 4 foot field fencing (woven wire with the 4 inch by 6 inch spaces between the strands) is very inexpensive, and goats will not put their heads through a pasture fence with the same stubborn redundancy that they will put their heads through the fence in a smaller pen. Housing and supplemental feeding have to be approached differently if the goats are going to live on the pasture, but the time to decide which way you want to fence is before you get started. I would recommend building at least a couple of pens, however. There is often someone that is sick, being bred, has new kids, or for some reason needs to be separate from the herd, so two or three pens will come in very handy.

If you have barbed wire around your pasture already, your best bet is to line it with four foot field fence or woven wire. Some people just add more strands of barbed wire, but the strands would have to be about 3 inches apart, and pretty tight, to dissuade a young goat. The goats that are the best escape artists are the young ones between three and eight months of age. As in all young things, these roughians seem to think they are indestructible and will tackle feats in the name of escape that would stump Houdini.

Many people have had very good luck with electric fences for their goats. To be effective, an electric fence needs to be at least four strands with the first strand about five inches from the ground, and quite hot. Once a goat has been shocked by a good electric fence, they are smart enough to stay clear. Even the young ones. But the minute the fence looses power, or shorts out, they can tell, and will go through it. I gave up using electric fences because the power where I live is too unstable. Of course, one solution to this problem would be solar powered fencers, if they are hot enough.

Another good option is the stiff panels that come in 12 to 16 foot lengths, and 3 to 5 foot heights. Again, the smaller the space between the strands, the better. However, even these will be bent in time if the posts are more than 8 foot apart, unless they are lined with electric fencing.

Fencing for Bucks

Keeping a big meat buck where he is supposed to be, during breeding season, can be a test of your creativity, as well as your engineering skills. A 250 pound buck can break a 2 by 6 piece of lumber without even exerting himself. The best fencing for bucks is a combination of several different fencing types, layered on top of each other.

Start your buck pen by building a solid base of either 2 inch pipe, or 2 by 6 lumber. Put 4 to 6 inch treated wooden posts (or 3 to 4 inch pipe) in the ground at a space of about 6 foot apart. Then add 2 by 6 wooden (or 2 inch pipe) cross bars starting 6 inches from the ground, then 18 inches, then 36 inches. Now cover this, on the buck's side of the fence, with 4 or 5 foot high stiff panels, or woven wire. Then, on the inside of the woven wire, add a strand of electric fencing at about 18 to 24 inches from the ground, and another at the top of the fence.

I know this may seem like 'over-kill', especially when you bring home that cute little 80 pound buck kid. But when he is 3 years old, and decides to go get that cute little thing wagging her tail at him, you will be glad you started right, honest.

Picture 6: A 250 pound buck can break a 2 by 6 without even exerting himself. [*]

Building a Quarantine Pen

If you continue to raise goats, you will eventually want a quarantine pen. Whenever you bring new animals onto the ranch, no matter how reliable the source, they should be quarantined for at least 3 weeks. The same is true when you bring your own animals home from a goat show. I know it doesn't seem like a big deal now, but the first time a new animal gives some nasty virus to your entire herd, you will be out building a quarantine pen.

This pen does not need to be large, although it does need to be escape proof. It should be at least 20 feet away from any of your other goats, in a spot where you are not going to need to house more goats later, and it should be downwind of the rest of your goats.

---

[*] This picture donated by Kids-R-Us Goat Farm in Uvalde, Texas.

Housing

Goats need a place to get out of the wind and the wet. How extensive this housing has to be depends on the climate in your area, the number of goats who are going to be sleeping there, and how much time they are going to have to spend inside.

If you are going to raise all your goats totally indoors, with no, or limited, access to the outside, you need to allow each goat at least 20 square feet of space. There are many areas where goat raisers have to bring their animals in for the winter because of climates that are too wet or impossibly cold. People in these areas need to plan to build large enough barns that the goats can be penned indoors. How you structure this barn, is entirely up to you. You will need to plan it in such a way that there are separate spaces for goats, feed, equipment and walking

Picture 7: . There are many areas where goat raisers have to bring their animals in for the winter because of climates that are too wet or impossibly cold. [*]

space. Another thing to consider, if you are building a barn, is installing a frostless faucet indoors. You will also want to put in conduit for electricity, and a telephone.

---

[*] This picture donated by Kids-R-Us Goat Farm in Uvalde, Texas.

People who don't put a telephone in the barn always live to regret it, especially when there is an emergency and you can't call the veterinarian from the barn.

Picture 8: . Structurally, the house can be anything that you like.[*]

If you are going to have your goats in pens, they will spend more time in their houses than they would if they were in a pasture. Under these conditions, plan to give them each at least 16 square feet of space. The houses should be in one corner of the pen, with the door to the house facing in the opposite direction from the wind. This is very important. It is more important than facing South for the sun, or whether or not you can see the goats from your house. If the weather can blow into the goat house, it will become a mire of manure, mud, and goats. Structurally, the house can be anything that you like. It needs to be at least 4 foot tall, enclosed on at least three sides, tight enough to keep the rain out, and big enough for the number of goats who are going to be sharing it.

If you are going to have the goats out on the pasture, you will want the goat house to be up close to your end of the pasture. This way the goats will come home and be more protected at night. As far as space, they really don't need very much, because they won't spend that much time in it. Probably 12 square feet per goat would be plenty. I raise Boer goats, and find that many of them put on such

[*] This picture donated by Kids-R-Us Goat Farm in Uvalde, Texas.

a dense winter coat that they won't even go into their houses unless the temperatures get below 0 degrees F, or extremely wet.

Goat houses can be made from almost anything. Those that are made from old pallets covered with plywood will only work if they are structurally very sound to begin with. The pallets will disintegrate over time, weakening the whole structure. Calf houses that are made for two or three calves work well. You just don't use the removable side. I know a rancher who has had very good luck with old plastic fertilizer tanks. He just cuts a door in one side, reinforces the door with 2 by 4's, and cuts out part of the floor so the house will drain. There are also companies that make some very nice portable huts that work well and look a little nicer, too.

Contrary to rumor, kid goats, even meat kids, will find a way to dance on your goat houses. When you are building, you should try to keep the houses at lease 4 feet away from all outside fences, just in case. You should also keep this in mind when positioning your wood pile, pallet storage, hay stack, etc.

One thing you might want to consider, is whether or not you can get into the house if there is an emergency. I once had a doe who kidded unexpectedly in one of our 4 foot tall goat houses. She had never kidded before, and was screaming and running around in circles dropping kids who were still in their sacks. When I rushed in to save the kids from suffocation, I had to dive under the 3 ½ foot high cross bar on the door, and threw out my knee. I got to the kids in time, but had to have help to get back out of that #@#@#!! house! I prefer 5 or 6 foot tall goat houses.

Kidding Pens

Most breeders use an area in the barn for kidding. I will be spending more time on kidding pens in the Chapter 7, "Kidding", but you need to be aware of the possible need if you are going to build facilities. A kidding pen is a small space, about 4 foot by 8 foot, where you can put your does to be alone when they are ready to kid. If you are building your barn, plan on building at least two kidding pens in one corner. You can even plan them in such a way that they can collapse when not in use and be stored along one wall.

Another thing to consider for your kidding area, is closed circuit television cabling. I know this sounds excessive, but if you are building your facilities, a conduit can be put in at the same time as your water lines, and electrical and telephone cable. Then, if you decide you are tired of running back and forth to the barn in the snow, a camera can be added for less than $500.

Picture 9: . For hay type feeds, a feeder that has a hay rack over a tray or trough works the best.[*]

Feeders

Goats have a tendency to pull their feed out of the feeder and play with it, walk on it, sleep on it. One of the challenges of a goat rancher is to provide the goats with feeders that don't allow them to waste the feed that we are so carefully providing for them. For hay type feeds, a feeder that has a hay rack over a tray or trough works the

---

[*] This picture donated by Hill Country Farms in Spicewood, Texas.

Picture 10: There are as many different feeders as there are people who design them.[*]

Picture 11: This feeder has 'keyhole' openings.[**]

[*] This picture donated by Hill Country Farms in Spicewood, Texas.
[**] This picture donated by Wynneshire Farm in Ridgefield, Washington.

best. The best ones that I have found are made for calves, but there are as many different types of feeders out there as there are people to design them.

Why can't we just throw the hay on the ground? For one thing, the goats will pick up worms from the ground when they eat the hay. They will also go to the bathroom on it, transferring disease to other goats and ruining their hay. One of the biggest frustrations for the new goat rancher, is that the little darlings just refuse to watch where they point their backsides when they are making goat pellets. They will even go in their waterers! Goats are very talented animals.

Picture 12: Kids love to sleep in feeders.[*]

When you are buying and positioning your feeders, you need to consider how you are going to fill the feeder. A person carrying hay or a bucket through a pasture full of hungry goats, is committing suicide. If your goats are in a pen, put the feeder near enough to the fence that you can reach over to feed. If your goats are in a large pasture,

---

[*] This picture donated by Nancy Coovert from Kimberly, Idaho.

use a series of feeders with the ends near the fence that is closest to the hay stack. You are probably better off with a series of feeders rather than one big one, because goats tend to try to 'guard' as much feed as they can, and one goat cannot 'guard' more than one side of one feeder at a time.

Alternatively, if your goats are in a pasture, you can use a large round bulk feeder to feed hay, or self-limiting supplements, automatically. This is harder to do, because it requires some extra planning to find a feed that will work for bulk feeding goats.

Waterers and Mineral Feeders.

When you are designing your pens and pasture fences, plan to put in water lines and electrical outlets. One of the first things my husband did when we started building facilities was install 1200 feet of water line, with conduit for electrical outlets, out by the goat houses. This allows you to put in waterers with frostless faucets, or even automatic waterers, and coinciding outdoor electrical outlets to plug in water heaters, heat lamps and power tools.

Waterers should be large enough to need filling only once a day. If you have 50 goats in the same pasture, you need about a 50 gallon waterer. Be careful to use low sided (12 inches or less) waterers so young goats can't fall in and drown. The water should be fresh every day, and in cold weather, the water must be heated. Goats will not drink enough water to stay healthy if they have to fight ice or filth.

When you design your facilities, don't forget salt and minerals. A mineral feeder can be anything from a plastic dog bowl to a specialized feeder with a wind fin to keep it facing away from the wind. Goats should have salt and minerals offered to them, either in block or loose form. One possible problem with block form, is that it allows for the exchange of disease if there are any goats using it that are unhealthy.

Working Corral

You should plan to have a place on your ranch where you can move your goats into a small pen to give shots and do any other work that involves handling the goats. A place in the fence that can have a stiff panel attached to make a V in the fence, to use like a funnel, is a great idea to get all your goats into your handling pen at one time. The pen itself can be V shaped with a squeeze chute at one end, if you like. Or it can just be a smaller pen, say 12 foot by 24 foot, where the goats can be crowded together so they can be caught and handled without chasing them. Goats don't respond well to being chased, or to being worked by dogs. If you can design facilities that allow you to be calm and in control when you need to handle your goats, you will be a much happier rancher.

Picture 13: A Great Pyranees Guard Dog.[*]

---

[*] This picture donated by Sand Creek Boer Goats from Shelly, Idaho.

Guard Animals

Predators can be a problem on any goat or sheep ranch. Cougars, bobcats, racoons, wild hogs, coyotes, foxes, and the neighborhood dogs can all cause losses. A good fence will be a big help toward discouraging many predators, but most ranchers want some kind of guard animal out with their stock too.

Picture 14: Donkeys and Llamas are both becoming popular as breeders find that these animals will eat the same feed as the goats, don't wander off, and don't chew on goat ears. *

For centuries, dogs have been guarding stock. A herding dog should not be used to guard livestock, because they're instincts for chasing the stock will get in the way. Some of the more popular guard dogs for goats include Anatolians, Great Pyranees, Komodors, Maremas and Tibetan Mastifs. To be a good guardian, the dog must be put out with the herd as a puppy so that it accepts the herd as 'family'. Training a dog as a guardian can be frustrating because all dogs go through a puppy stage when they must be taught what behavior is or is not acceptable. They must

---

* This picture from Bowman Boer Ranch from Twin Falls, Idaho.

be taught not to chew on goat ears, or hooves, and not to stray outside the domain of the pasture.

More recently, people have been experimenting with different kinds of livestock to guard their flocks. Donkeys and Llamas are both becoming popular as breeders find that these animals will eat the same feed as the goats, don't wander off, and don't chew on goat ears. However, these too can have other unpleasant habits. Both donkeys and llamas should be castrated males, or females. An intact male can be too aggressive, and, in the case of llamas, may be sexually attracted to your goats. Male or female donkeys may severely injure goats when they are eating feed and the goats try to share the meal. A female guard animal with a baby would be somewhat distracted from the job at hand, and might be aggressive toward any goats who come too close. Both donkeys and llamas sound an alarm when danger is near, and both will trample an intruding predator.

Picture 15: Goat kids make friends easily with other animals.[*]

As in everything, I would recommend that you do some research, and talk to breeders and owners of the animals

[*] This picture donated by Kids-R-Us Goat Farm in Uvalde, Texas.

you are considering, before you make a decision on a guard animal for your herd.

NOTES:

BABY GOATS FOR SALE TODAY!

4

Buying your First Goats

You are now ready to start considering your first goat purchase. You have read Chapter 2 and know what you want to do with your goats and why. You know whether you want to raise breeding stock, or strictly meat production stock, or some combination in between. This is my favorite part too, but let's think for just one more moment. Do you have a place to put your animals when you get them home? Are your fences up to the challenge? If it's almost winter, have you built a shelter for your new additions? Do you have the phone number of a good veterinarian or experienced goat raiser handy? Do you have something to feed them when they get off the truck? Yes to all the above? Great! Let's go find some goats!

The very first and most important thing I tell people is "Don't buy at the auctions and sale yards!" No matter what you are going to do with your stock, a healthy goat will grow and produce better than a sick animal. It has been my experience that auctions are a good place to get rid of problem animals, and a perfect place to acquire someone else's problems. Think about it. Why would a reputable breeder sell his animals at auction, where he has no control over price, if he could sell them by private treaty? Unless, he needed money fast, or didn't want to damage his reputation because there was some problem with the goats. Whether you are looking for good foundation stock, or good fullblood breeding stock, the answer is the same: Find a reputable breeder!

How do you find that reputable breeder? Talk to the goat people in your area. Even if that ranch you pass by every day on your way home from work only has dairy goats, there is a good chance that they know who in the area is raising meat type animals. So stop by one night on the way home. There is nothing a goat rancher likes to talk about better than his goats!

Another important place to look for goats is the local classified ads and/or any farm paper that serves your area. If people have animals to sell, they will be in the classified ads sooner or later. You can also call the goat associations. Most areas of the country have local dairy goat associations, and I list several meat, Boer goat, Fainting Goat and Kiko goat associations in the "Resources" section of this book. Give them a call. There are probably more meat goat raisers in your area than you realize.

Once you have made contact with some local breeders, be sure to shop around. Most breeders are trying to do their very best to raise good, healthy animals. However, if you don't look at several ranches, you won't have an opportunity to decide which goats appeal to you, or pinpoint why that last place just didn't "feel" right. If at all possible, take a knowledgeable advisor with you to keep your reputable breeder reputable.

Buying Fullbloods

Once you have found fullblood breeding stock, what do you look for? First, look at the ranch. Is it well kept or does it have junk lying all over the pasture? No one's ranch shows like a page out of Home and Garden, but most serious breeders try to keep the mess down to a minimum and certainly away from anyplace that the goats could get hurt on it. Is your breeder happy to show you a lot of animals, or does he have one set aside for you to look at. Breeders who only want to show me one goat always make me curious to know what is wrong with the rest of the herd, or why he doesn't want me to compare them to the goat he has for sale.

Picture 16: A Fainting Goat doe.[*]

Take a look at the animals. Are they well fed? Do they have clean waterers? Ask your breeder about his feed program. Does he have other goats that are related to the goats he is showing you? Can you see the parents? What about brothers and sisters? Does he line breed or is he out crossing? Inbreeding is generally accepted in livestock breeding circles, up to an extent, and only if you know what you are doing. Although "line breeding" can be used to strengthen positive attributes, it can just as easily strengthen faults. Plus, the original Boers were often so inbred, because the seed stock was so small, that I find any avoidable inbreeding to be unadvisable.

---

[*] This picture donated by Phil Sponenberg from Blacksburg, Virginia

Don't be afraid to ask questions. If the breeder is serious about his breeding program, and proud of his goats, you probably won't be able to shut him up. Besides, the only way for you to get an impression of his knowledge, honesty and integrity is if you talk to him!

Another important area to discuss with your breeder is his disease prevention program. Does he do any testing? Does he vaccinate? What kind of wormer works best in his area? Does he keep medical records? Maybe there are some other animals he would be willing to sell? How do the prices on those other animals compare with the animal he is offering you?

Remember, you can buy a Fullblood meat goat for next to nothing, but you will probably get what you paid for. Someone who is watching their bloodlines and is a serious breeder is going to know that their stock is worth more, and will probably be charging for it. That is not to say that an animal is a gem just because he carries a big price tag! The animal business is just like any other business. Although most breeders love their animals and are trying to do a good job, there are people who will charge inflated prices for poor animals and sleep just fine at night while you go broke. Your best protection is education. That is why you must know how to spot a good animal, get to know your breeder, check his reputation, and get knowledgeable advice if you can find it.

Registration & Fullblood Meat Goats

All fullblood Kikos, Boers and Fainting goats are registerable. If there is some reason that the breeder you are speaking with can't or won't produce registration papers, there may be a problem with the goat or the way he acquired the goat. Registration papers are the only way you have of being sure that the goat you take home is the goat you understood you were paying for.

Of course, it may be that the three month old kid you are looking at just hasn't been registered yet. Or that that breeder doesn't register his buck kids until they are a year old, or are sold. Even in these circumstances, however, a fullblood goat breeder should be able to produce registration papers on the parents, and fill you out a registration form on that kid - on the spot. Even if he is traveling. Why would a reputable breeder take goats on the road that are for sale, and not take their papers?

A Boer goat that originated from pure Boer parents is called a Fullblood. If a breeder has started with a fullblood Boer buck and bred to some other kind of goat the resulting offspring are called "half bloods". Even half blood Boers (and Kikos or Tennessee Fainting goats) are registerable as long as the father was a fullblood or a purebred. By breeding a half blood to a fullblood you get a three-quarter. Then by breeding the three-quarter to a fullblood again, you get a seven-eighths, etc. When you get to 15/16 or 31/32 you have an "American purebred". The offspring of these animals will never be called "fullblood" no matter how many generations you continue to breed back to a fullblood. With Boers, however, an American purebred is entitled to show in the same class as is a fullblood, and progeny from an American purebred crossed with some other kind of goat are called half bloods and are registerable. For the purposes of this book, I will refer to all American purebred and fullblood stock from here forward as "fullblood".

Fullblood Boer Bloodlines

At the time of this printing, there have been several large foreign producers in the fullblood Boer goat industry. Each of these producers have become a "blood line" in themselves by virtue of the number of goats they have produced and exported into the United States and Canada. The two largest of these early producers were the first to send huge numbers of goats into the western markets. Therefore, their goats now constitute the least sought after blood lines. I am not saying that the goats from these blood lines are any less desirable, but rather that people are currently tired of them.

If you want to raise fullblood Boer goat breeding stock, it is important to know the blood line you are buying as well as the health and quality of the animal. If the bloodline you are buying is one of the latest to come into this country, it is possible that the market price will be higher, for a while.

Within a very few years, it will be much less important which foreign ranch's blood lines your Boer goat carries, because most of the animals in the West will have pedigrees full of western registration numbers. It will be much harder to trace foreign blood lines. So don't get so hung up on blood lines that you forget to buy the style and conformation that appeals to you, conforms to your stated goals and fits your needs. For instance, a meat production herd does not really need a fullblood buck that has perfect (or even good) color. Another borderline area, is the number of teats a Boer has. These animals came from South Africa, originally, with four teats. Many people are not comfortable with that characteristic in their fullbloods. However, if you are producing meat, and the teats work, why would you pay more for a two teated buck? I would not suggest skimping on the length or width of your meat production buck, however. A broad chest, long loin and deep muscling are all attributes you are going to need in your meat kids.

How do I Start my Meat Herd?

The biggest question on the minds of people wanting to start a meat production herd is, "How much do I need to invest to get started?" Although there are many factors to be considered, and many of these were covered Chapter 2, you can usually expect to find good does for your foundation stock for between $50 and $150 per doe. How many you buy will depend on the depth of your pocket and your available graze and/or feed. In general, you will also need to purchase at least one good fullblood meat buck (Boer, Tennessee, Kiko, etc.). Your bucks will probably cost you between $500 and $2,000 each. The breed you choose will depend on what is available in your area and which breed you prefer.

As far as which breed of goat to look for when you go shopping for your foundation does, I would recommend

Boer crosses, but the prices usually make them untenable financially. It has been said that Spanish, or southern "scrub" goats are probably the most cost effective. That's if you live in the Southern United States and know where you can find some healthy Spanish goats. Another good choice might be Angoras, if you know someone willing to sell a large number of older, larger does. There are also meat type Nubians, or mixed breed goats with some meat goat or angora in their lineage, if you happen to find some for prices you can afford. Usually, a meat production herd is made up of a mixture of the animals that are locally available, and often that means just plain dairy goats. Which is really OK. I've known many a wonderful Plain Jane who gets out there and produces like crazy!

One thing that is <u>not</u> important for the foundation does in your meat production herd, is registration papers. A crossbreed doe will produce meat just as well as a carefully bred, registered animal. Whether or not you need registration papers on your fullblood bucks is another issue. If I am going to spend a lot of money on a breeding animal because his blood lines suggest that he has the characteristics I am looking for, whether he is a registered Angus bull or a fullblood meat buck, I am going to want a piece of paper that tells me I got what I paid for. Also, if I want to sell this buck in three years, he will sell better with papers. However, if my next door neighbor has been raising these goats for several years, and I have been watching them over the fence, I would probably be more interested in getting a discount on that buck kid that I saw born last year, in exchange for not receiving papers. Even still, I would want to be sure that the father was the one that I have been admiring in the pasture, and not some visiting imposter, perhaps boarded for the night. And I would want copies of the registration papers on the parents. In other words, I like things in writing. If you don't need that reassurance, that makes you a more secure person than I am.

What to look for in a Meat Goat

Whether you are buying full bloods, meat foundation goats, half bloods or evaluating your own kids, it is important to know what you're looking for. The best way to learn to identify good meaty animals is to take a class or have an expert carefully teach you what to look for. Several of the associations hold regular classes all over the continent. Give them a call and see if they have anything coming up in your area!

When selecting meat goats, several criteria should be considered: conformation (structural correctness), general appearance (size, depth and width of body, and muscling), health, and condition. I will try to explain each area to you, at least briefly, so you can begin to judge your goats for yourself.

Conformation is the symmetrical formation and arrangement of the parts of your goat. (Please refer to the drawing at the end of Chapter 1.) A good meat goat should be balanced in appearance from the side with straight, level top (the back) and bottom lines. In other words, he should look like a good block of wood. The length of the back (loin) is very important to the market desirability of a meat goat since the loin is the most expensive section of the meat. The loin starts just behind the ribs and includes the top of the back, on both sides of the spine, all the way back to the rump. The loin can be described in 3 ways; length, width and depth. Some animals can have a long loin, but with very little width, depth or meat on it. The rump should be nearly level from the hips to the tail over a muscular thigh. The barrel should be large in depth, length and breadth to show that the animal can contain a large rumen, and will be able to sustain itself on forage. Extremely "pot bellied" animals are not a plus. The 'heart girth' should also be broad with ribs that are well sprung.

The legs should be straight when viewed from the front or the back. The rear legs should be perpendicular from the heel to the hock, and have a definite angle to them from the hock to the stifle joint, when viewed from the side.

Muscling should come well down on both the front and rear legs. The chest should be deep and broad and the rear legs should be set far enough apart to accommodate a good udder (even in bucks, since bucks sire doe kids and will pass on this attribute to their daughters).

The general appearance of the goat should be one of balance, health and strength. We are not looking for fine bones and dairy character from these animals at all! Even a good half blood doe needs to be thick and heavy looking, not a wirey, lightweight little sweetheart perched at the top of long skinny legs. And you are definitely not looking for a huge, hanging udder! Most meat herds are raised on large pastures containing lots of scrub and brush. No one is going to go out there every day and make sure that udder is in good condition and getting milked enough for the doe's best health. Look for animals that appear as though they could raise kids on very little feed, and with very little help.

The eyes should be bright and the forehead should be broad. A thin animal with a poor coat and dull eyes will make a poor addition to your herd, while a robust, muscular animal will produce kids with like attributes. Look for muscling in the rear legs, buttocks, outside and inside of the thigh, shoulders, chest and neck.

The health of a goat is not always easy to establish because many diseases do not have obvious symptoms. A healthy goat is alert, with bright eyes and a good coat. A goat in poor health has a rough coat, is listless with dull eyes, or is possibly too thin. The best indication to the general health of a particular animal is sometimes the overall appearance of the herd she comes from. Of course, we are all trying to look for animals with no obvious problems, but what about the problems that are not as obvious? The best solution is usually to talk to the breeder about his health program. Does he worm and vaccinate his goats regularly? Does he keep health records of any kind? What does he do about abscesses? Does he have any does with arthritic problems? Do his does have any trouble raising their kids out to weaning age?   Do the animals in his area ever have any trouble with foot conditions?   What is the average birth weight?

Picture 17:   The general appearance of the goat should be one of balance, health and strength.[*]

The "condition" of the goat refers to the amount of fat the animal is carrying.   Meat goat judges disagree widely in this area, but if you are buying a breeding animal it should have no more than a reasonable amount of fat. Meat goats tend to look "fat" to us because they are so much thicker than dairy goats.   If a meat animal is too fat, it will be obvious to you - it will be rotund!   Remember, an over conditioned, fat doe will have fat deposits around her ovaries and will not breed as easily as a doe with a

---

[*] This picture donated by Shep Land and Livestock from Council, Idaho.

reasonable amount of fat for her breed. By the same token, an extremely thin doe (or buck) probably has some internal problem and may not be able to survive on rough feed or provide enough nutrition for growing kids.[13]

Picture 18: Three year old Kiko does.[*]

How to Choose a Doe

Whether you are wanting to raise breeding stock or develop a meat production herd, you will need to buy a majority of does. Most breeding stock producers start with a fullblood buck, a few fullblood does and 20 or 30 does of some other breed to produce cross breeds. A meat production herd will be looking for 25 to 50 females for every buck. So what do you look for in your doe?

Try to find stock between 10 months and 36 months of age. Does that have kidded at least once are less of a risk because you know they are fertile. Ask the breeder why he is selling these particular does. They may have a weakness that is important to him, for his breeding program, but not important to a meat herd. I once bought a big, beautiful dairy doe that produced triplets every year,

---

[*] This picture donated by Lillie Hill Farms Meat Goats from Lincoln, California.

but the owner was culling her because she milked heavily for only three months after kidding, and then dried up. This was a disaster for his dairy herd, but perfect for my meat herd. I want her to kid easily, raise her kids with little or no help from me, then dry off as quickly as possible.

Picture 19: A herd of Kiko and Kiko-cross doelings. *

Ask the breeder how these does kidded last year. An evasive answer should make you question both the purchase of these animals, and the integrity of this breeder. If these are your first goats, it is important to get stock that have as few inherent problems as possible.

Look for does with apparently sound udders with one (or two in Boers) average size teats on each side. A goat's udder is very important even if you are not milking your goats. That udder is going to be the milk bottle for her kids! So take another look. Udders should not be lop-sided or lumpy. They should not be dragging on the ground or have teats that stick out on the sides so the

---

* This picture donated by Caston Creek Ranch from Wister, Oklahoma.

kids can't find them. If the doe has more than one orifice on each teat, the milk can run out of the orifice the kid is not using, and right up his nose! On fullblood Boers or Boer crosses, it is acceptable to have two teats on each side as long as they are not so close together as to become one teat with two orifices.

Look for healthy animals with good coats, that are of adequate size (teeny, frail looking little does will not kid out well!) and free of obvious deformities. Buying a herd of only "virgin" doelings has been likened to having a semi-death wish! Although this might be putting it a little strongly, doelings do have more problems kidding. If you have to buy virgin does be sure they are going to be at least 70 to 80 pounds at breeding age. I prefer to breed a doeling after she is 8 or 9 months old so she has time to get a little bit bigger. Also, virgin does have not kidded yet, so you can not tell if they will have had udders, be poor mothers or have fertility problems. [14]

When I was getting started, I bought a collection of dairy does from several ranches, all of whom were supposed to be pregnant. I was not offered a choice, but took what they loaded in my truck. I didn't know enough to ask questions about kidding history or health. They were goats and they looked OK to me. Out of 12 goats, two were infertile, two had very serious kidding problems and most of the rest were diseased. I ended up getting rid of the whole lot and starting over. The next time, I went shopping. I asked around. I toured the ranches, asked to see parents, kids and siblings, discussed kidding tendencies and disease control programs. Although I bought only "virgin" does the second time, they were all big girls out of big healthy moms who were bred for low disease, high multiple births (their mothers always had three) and kidding ease. Every one of them kidded beautifully, all by themselves, and still do.

If you are going to start raising a small herd of fullblood meat goats, you really do not need to buy a buck the very first year. Buy at least two bred does so that they will have a "buddy"! Buy them pregnant with an ultrasound certificate, registration papers, service memo, and health records. If you buy at least two that are from the same herd, they will already be bonded.

Good conformation and features are very important when buying your does. Don't fall into the trap of buying does just because they are offered to you. Even a meat production herd needs does that are going to throw meaty kids rather than skinny spindly ones. If you are raising fullbloods, then you need to look at that doe as the mother of your future generations. Is that the way you want your goats to look in the years to come?

Bucks

Picture 20: Overall, your buck should be a big, strong "macho" kind of animal.[*]

The decision to buy a fullblood meat buck is a difficult one for many people. Boer and Kiko bucks can get to weigh upwards of 350 pounds! They can be very hard on fences and goat houses at that size, and although Boer bucks tend to have very mild temperaments, those horns must be respected. However, if you are going to have a serious

---

[*] This picture from Bowman Boer Ranch in Twin Falls, Idaho.

breeding program, and unless you're a real wiz at AI, or you have a great agreement with a neighbor who owns a meat buck, you're stuck with buying a buck.

My advice? A cheap buck might be easier to swallow at first, but in the end he'll most likely choke your pocket book. If you can buy a buck for way under market price stop and ask yourself, "What does the breeder know about him or his father that I don't know?" Even in a meat herd, a buck that is going to produce small, low gaining kids, serious flaws, or no kids at all, is not a smart buy. Everything produced on your ranch, probably forever (considering that even after the buck has moved on, you are still breeding his daughters and producing his grand kids and great-grand kids!), is going to be related to that buck. A doe might influence a portion of your herd, but your buck will "touch" them all. So look for a good buck that is priced reasonably for the market, and don't settle for the one that will be the easiest on your budget.

The best bet is always an older, proven buck. That way you can see some of his kids, obtain kidding records, etc. Unfortunately, older bucks are more expensive and hard to find. They are also a little intimidating. Most new goat raisers would much rather buy a kid and "grow up with him" than start out with a full grown buck. If you do find an older buck that you really love, and you love the kids you're seeing out of him, you feel that your fences are up to the challenge, and he throws the percentage of doe and buck kids you had in mind (Remember: the doe determines the number of kids and the buck determines the sex.) then, by all means, don't walk away! Buy him!

For the rest of us who have to make do with an unproven kid, check his pedigree. How inbred is he? Check his bloodlines. Are his father and mother there for you to see? Check his conformation! You are looking for a broad chest, broad escutcheon (space between his back legs), a long, straight back, straight legs from the front and back views, a good angle to his back legs from the side, strong feet, a deep strong rib cage with a good spring to it, a strong neck and head, and a wide horn set. Overall, your buck should be a big, strong "macho" kind of animal.

NOTES:

Feeding for Production

Goats will find nutrition in places that cattle cannot. That is because a goat will sample everything. They will eat the trees, the weeds, the sagebrush, the grass, and even the fence posts. However, the nutrition has to be there for them to find. If a small herd of goats is roaming a 600 acre patch of rough ground, but that ground has good nutritious vegetation growing on it, the goats will go find it. The thing that a goat, or any other animal, can't do, is manufacture basic nutritional elements that do not exist in the feeds that are available.

Goat raising can be a profitable business, *but you can not starve a profit out of any animal.* An animal that is not properly fed will not grow as fast, reproduce as well, stay as healthy, or reach its genetic potential. Goats are incredibly adaptable and can digest many types of feeds that other animals cannot. What you will feed your goats probably depends on what is available in your area for a reasonable price. However, understanding the nutritional elements that are present in that reasonably priced feed, so that you can supplement your goat's diet with the nutrients that will help them to grow and produce, only makes sense.

Becoming knowledgeable about the feeds you are using, or the pasture you are grazing on, will allow you to get the maximum profit out of your goat ranch, and you will no longer be at the mercy of the feed store salesman. It is important to understand what we are spending our feed dollars on, so that we can spend them to the greatest effect. Feeding our goats too much protein, or too much energy just because the salesman said it was goat feed, is an expensive way to put those nutrients back into the soil on our ranch. Because that is exactly where they are going to go. The goats will just flush them through their bodies and onto the ground.

Digestion in Ruminants

Goats are ruminants. They have four stomachs. Because of their digestive system, ruminants can manufacture many of the vitamins and some of the protein amino acids that have to be fed to simple-stomached animals. They can also readily digest large quantities of roughage. The rumen is the first and largest section of the digestive system, the storage tank. While the feed is in the rumen it will be regurgitated and re-chewed as 'cud' to help complete the digestive process. A goat can chew 20 gallons of cud in a day!

After the feed leaves the rumen it passes through the reticulum, the omasum and the abomasum, then finally through into the small intestines where the digestive process is completed.

What do I feed my Goats?

Goats are foragers and browsers, as opposed to grazers. They will eat the bark off the trees, and the leaves off the bushes before they will eat grass. That is one of the things that attracts some people to goat raising. Goats like to eat weeds. However, a goat has to eat a lot of fresh, growing plant matter to get the amount of dry matter she needs to breed and raise her kids. If your goats are feeding themselves out there on the pasture, you just need to be sure that they have a high enough quality forage available to them to do what they need to be doing to make you a profit. It would be unusual forage that allowed a doe, for instance, to produce enough milk for two kids, without any supplementation in the way of grain products from you. That doesn't mean it isn't possible, just that it would be unusual.

Generally, you can raise about 6 goats to one acre of good pasture/browse. Goats love to eat tree bark and will kill young (sometimes even older) trees. By the end of this chapter I hope you will feel comfortable about going out into your pasture and finding out what kind of nutritional elements are, or are not, available in that pasture. Then, you can reasonably feed extra, or supplemental, feeds that will fulfill the needs of your goats, not the expectations of the neighbors, feed salesman, or the dairy down the road.

Most of us have to feed a full ration to our goats at least part of the year. If you don't have much browse available for your goats, you need to be ready to provide for that ration most of the year, or maybe all year long. Again, you can't starve a profit out of your goats. So what should you look for to make up that full ration?

People have different things available depending on where they live. I happen to have alfalfa available to me at about $80.00 a ton. I can also purchase a complete pelletized feed for about $200.00 a ton. As an example, If I am going to feed alfalfa hay to 50 goats, all year around, I would plan for each goat to eat about 4 pounds a day. Goats tend to waste a huge amount of alfalfa hay because of the nature of the hay. It has stems and little leaves. The goats tend to shake out the hay and lose most of the leaves onto the ground, or back into the feeder where it gets wet, or compressed. So, even though they only need to take in about 4 pounds, I would probably plan on feeding more. But for the purposes of this discussion, let's use 4 pounds. 4 pounds times 50 goats = 200 pounds a day. Times 365 days in a year = 73000 lbs. a year, or 36.5 tons. That is a lot of alfalfa! But alfalfa is a very nutritious feed. It is really more than my dry does who have weaned their kids or are newly pregnant are going to need. It is also less than my lactating does are going to need. I would be looking for ways to cut my costs by putting my dry does out on pasture for part of the year. I would also be looking into the different supplements available to me for the times that I need more energy or protein in my ration, like for the lactating moms.

Just as a matter of comparison, I would only have to feed 3 pounds of that complete pelletized feed to my goats a day. 3 times 50 = 150 pounds a day. 150 times 365 days = 54750 lbs. per year, or 27 tons. With this I would have to supplement with some long stem feed (hay) to keep their rumens working, but only about a pound a day per goat, and it would not have to be alfalfa because the nutrition would be coming from the pellets. I would also not have to supplement my lactating does. So which feed is cheaper for me? 37 tons alfalfa hay times $80.00 a ton = $2,900. 27 tons of pellets times $200 a ton = $5,475. Any contest?

I can also buy oat hay in my area for about $60.00 a ton. However, in this area, we harvest hay in July through September and it has to last us until next July. Oat hay loses its nutritional content and palatability in about 60 days. The rest of the year my goats would be eating straw.

Another thing to consider when you decide how to feed your goats, is how much you expect to be able to sell your kids for. If you are expecting your market to be about $75 per kid, then you really need to have some good pasture available to you for at least 5 months of the year. Even here in the Northwestern United States we can expect to have good pasture from about April 15th through at least the end of August, or mid September. That is 5 months that I only need to supplement my goats as needed for the stage of pregnancy, growth and kid raising they are in.

If, on the other hand, if you are expecting to get at least $250 to $750 for each of those kids, and you don't have a good labor force to help with the feeding, you might be more interested in that pelletized feed just for the simplicity of it.

On the northwest coast and in the Midwestern United States goat ranchers feed timothy hay. In Georgia, I have heard that they feed peanut hay. In Texas they feed Sudan hay, fertilized coastal hay, and red top cane hay. I know various people that feed their goats dried peas, corn stalks, onions, peanuts and banana peels. If something is available in your area, do the research. Find out what the nutritional value of that feed is, and whether or not it is harmful to goats. However, if there is no nutritional value, don't throw it to the goats just to fill their stomachs and make yourself feel like you've fed them. It isn't worth the effort. Go and find a feed that will accomplish your goals, both financially and for the nutritional health of your goats.

How Often should I Feed?

Goat ranching is as individual as the ranchers who do it. Everyone has a different schedule and a different labor force. Goats, especially meat goats, are very easy going and adaptable. They pretty much need to have something for their rumen to work on all the time, though. So it is a good idea to feed twice a day. You should always try to feed at the same time of day because the goats will get used to the routine. Just like everyone else, they like to have a set routine.

What if you work a crazy schedule and can only feed your goats at 8:00 A.M. on Mondays and Fridays and at 11:00 A.M. the rest of the week? The goats will just be happy to see you coming, and they will adapt. Try to feed them enough roughage that they will have something left over to munch on between meals, so their rumens stay active and healthy. However, if you are even later one day, and the goats aren't at the fence to meet you, you might look in the neighbor's flower garden. Goats are intelligent and creative.

Finding Out about Our Feeds

Feeding animals is a matter of simple nutrition. Most parents can look at a table full of food and tell you what nutritional elements are missing. We have been trained to look for the basic food groups; protein, starch, dairy products, and fruits and vegetables. Feeding goats is no different. You should be able to visualize what they are eating and tell what is missing. As my nutritionist is so fond of telling me, "Gail, this is not rocket science." I am going to try to explain good, basic goat nutrition and hope that I have not made it into rocket science.

Your job is to go out and explore the area that your goats live in. If it is a ½ acre pen, then you will need to go to the hay stack and the feed bins, or to your feed supplier to find out what is in your feeds. But if your goats live in a 600 acre pasture, you may need to take a sample bag with you so that you can find out exactly what your goats have available to eat. Remember that different things grow and are edible at different times of the year, too.

We have established that in different areas of the country different feeds are available to us. To find out the exact nutritional components of the hay type feed that is available to you to buy, or the feed that is growing in your pasture, you can start by calling your local county extension agent. Also, if there is a company in your area that manufactures feeds, you can call and talk to their nutritionist. These nutritionists need to know about the feeds in their area so that they can make supplements to go with them. If the first one isn't helpful, don't give up. I called 3 companies before I found someone to help, but he helped me to find out everything I wanted to know. You can also talk to your veterinarian. He may be able to help you find someone who can help you with your feeds.

You can also look at the list at the end of this chapter and try to figure it out for yourself. Remember, though, the exact feeds in these lists may not represent the same feeds as your neighbor grows in his field. We need to have guidelines, however, and this is a good place to start.

The Nutritional Requirements of Goats

The following discussion about nutrition is on a very basic level. If you are interested in knowing more about the nutritional requirements of your goats, I would like to encourage you to look into it further. There is a book you can buy called <u>Nutrient Requirements of Goats: Angora, Dairy and Meat Goats in Temperate and Tropical Countries </u>by the National Academy Press, Washington, D.C. 1981. Library of Congress # 81-84592. It is available from National Academy Press, 2101 Constitution Ave N.W., Washington, D.C. 20418. I would highly recommend it to you.

According to this book, the basic maintenance requirements of goats under no stress, who are not growing or lactating, who need no energy to keep warm, who are not traveling to get food, and who weigh 110 pounds, are:

	DM (lbs)	TDN (g)	TCP (g)	% TCP	Ca (g)	P (g)
110 lb (50kg) Dry Doe/ Buck	3 lbs	928g	110g	9.24%	4g	2.8g

No wait! Come back! This isn't hard, and it is only 5 things to learn. There are more nutrients in the tables, of course, but these are the ones we are going to focus on. So lets start at the top.

<u>DM (lbs)</u>: This translates, Dry Matter in pounds. Dry matter is how much food your goat is actually getting after you take out the water. In other words, if you turned your hay into absolutely dry powder, that would be the dry matter in the hay. All the nutrition tables are in terms of dry matter and percentages of dry matter because you aren't trying to measure the nutrition in the water in a pound of alfalfa. You are trying to measure the nutrition in the dry food part of a pound of alfalfa. This table tells us that your doe needs 3 pounds of dry matter a day to make her comfortable. That would probably work out to about 4 pounds of actual hay.

TDN (g): This stands for Total Digestible Nutrients in grams. This is one of four different gauges that are used for judging the energy in our feeds. The other three are DE or digestible energy, ME or metabolizable energy, and NE for net energy. The four methods of measurement are closely interrelated, and one can be derived from the others. TDN is measured in kgs and DE, NE and ME are measured in Mcals. Just in case you are interested, 1kg TDN = 1.109 Mcal DE, and 5.082 Mcal DE = 2.356 kcal NE. There will be a test later.

We will use TDN for the purposes of this book. Energy is a vital factor in goat nutrition. We must not forget energy in our quest for protein. Everything your goats do affects their energy needs. Energy can be increased by adding starches, grains, proteins and fats to your goat's diet. To a limited extent, energy can be translated 'sugar'. Goats require extra energy to stay warm, _grow_, lactate, be pregnant, walk from the barn to the back 40, even to grow hair. When we start figuring feed rations later in the chapter, keep in mind that these rations do not take into account _anything_ that may be costing your goats extra energy. If it is cold outside, you need to figure on more feed. If you live at a high altitude, or the pasture is at all large, you need to figure on more feed.

TCP (g): This translates Total Crude Protein in grams. This is the figure that we will use later on to derive our percentages of protein. Proteins are the basic building blocks of all animal cells. The protein requirements of animals are figured in calorie (energy) to protein ratios. So the two are very closely tied. Animals whose protein requirements are not being met will experience poor growth rates, low birth rates, poor milk production, and poor health. If the protein that your goat needs is not present in her feed, she will take it from her own muscles, blood and liver.

%TCP is the percentage of Total Crude Protein to dry matter that your animals require. This percentage is thrown way off if there is a lot of water in the feed, as in the case of fresh grass (as we will see in our example later). To figure percentage of total protein, multiply the percentage of protein for each type of feed, by the pounds of that feed. Then average:

If alfalfa hay is 16.2 % protein
and corn is 9.5 % protein
and barley is 11.9 % protein and you are planning to feed 4 pounds alfalfa, ½ pound corn and ½ pound barley, you would multiply:

4 lbs of alfalfa at 16.2= 64.8
½ lb of corn at 9.5 = 4.75
+½ lb of barley at 11.9 = + 5.95
=5 lbs of feed = 75.50

Now divide 75.50 by 5 lbs of total feed = 15.1 % protein

Ca (g): Calcium is a vital element for the health of your goats. Kids cannot grow and make strong bones without it, and lactating does will not be able to produce milk if their calcium requirements are not met. Calcium interacts with other minerals in your goats' diet to maintain a healthy animal.

P (g): Phosphorus is another vital mineral that is required for growth and milk production. The ratio of calcium to phosphorus in your goats' overall diet is extremely important to prevent urinary calculi buildup. The ratio of calcium to phosphorus should not be allowed to drop below 1.2 (calcium) to 1 (phosphorus).

OK. That wasn't too bad. We learned that our 110 pound doe who is being fed in a pen, and is not pregnant or lactating, needs 3 pounds a day of dry matter. That probably translates to about 4 pounds of dried feed because most of our feeds are about 85% to 90% dry matter, and the rest is water. Her feed also needs to have a reasonable amount of energy (carbohydrate), some basic minerals, and be about 9% protein.

Standards

Now, let's put all this into a standardized table that you can copy and take with you. These standards are from the government study, and are for goats who live in moderate climates and are not traveling very far for their feed, or under unusual stress conditions.[15] *These tables are nutritional requirements per one day.*

	DM (lbs)	TDN (g)	TCP (g)	% TCP	Ca (g)	P (g)
110 lb (50kg) Dry Doe/ Buck	3 lbs	928g	110g	9.24%	4g	2.8g
110 lb (50 kg) Doe in late Pregnancy	4 lbs	1192g	192g	10.8%	6g	4.2g
110 lb (50 kg) Doe – Lactating	4.8 lbs	1833g	326g	14.9%	13g	9.1g
66 lb (30 kg) Kid + .5 lb / day	3 lbs	943g	130g	9.5%	6g	4.2g

Dry Doe or a Buck: As we have already discussed, a dry doe is one who is not sick, lactating, or in late pregnancy, and, to fit into our table, who weighs 110 pounds. This standard also applies to bucks who are not growing or out breeding the girls. If they weigh 110 pounds. What if your animal weighs 220 pounds? The numbers do not go up in a perfectly straight line, so I will give you more tables so you can make reasonable estimates:

	DM (lbs)	TDN (g)	TCP (g)	% TCP	Ca (g)	P (g)
110 lb (50kg) Dry Doe/ Buck	3 lbs	928g	110g	9.24%	4g	2.8g
176 lb (80kg) Dry Doe/ Buck	3.75 lbs	1131g	156g	9.24%	6g	4.2g
220 lb (100kg) Dry Doe/ Buck	4.5 lbs	1336g	184g	9.24%	7g	4.9g

Doe in Late Pregnancy: A doe in late pregnancy is defined as a doe in the last 2 ½ months of pregnancy. Does do not need as much energy before they are bred, or in the first half of their pregnancy, and if they are getting it anyway, they can put on extra weight. Too much weight in a dry doe can cause her to put on fat around her ovaries, so when it is time to breed she may not produce as many eggs.

I have heard that breeding animals should be given extra energy when they are actually breeding. Studies have shown that giving the doe a little extra energy starting a couple weeks before you want to breed, may actually increase her fertility. Of course, you can't do that if you are already graining her. I would recommend reducing or eliminating the amount of grain you are feeding your dry does during the summer and early fall. Then increasing it to about 1 pound of grain a day, two weeks before you want to breed. (Always be careful not to change feeds too fast.) Then, once you have your girls bred, you can slack off again until they are half way through their pregnancy, then start increasing them over time. Usually, one or two pounds a day of a grain supplement will fill in the holes in the ration for a pregnant doe. Again, the numbers for the larger does don't go up in a straight line, so here is that table for a 176 pound doe:

	DM (lbs)	TDN (g)	TCP(g)	% TCP	Ca (g)	P (g)
110 lb (50 kg) Doe in late Pregnancy	4 lbs	1192g	192g	10.8%	6g	4.2g
176 lb (80 kg) Doe in Late Pregnancy	5 lbs	1528g	238g	10.8%	8g	5.6g

Lactating Doe: I figured this ration on the basis of a 110 pound animal who is producing 6.6 pounds of milk a day at 4% milk fat. As you can see, there are a lot of variables here to change on us. A dairy goat may produce quite a bit more than 6 pounds of milk a day, but we are talking about a meat goat. 6.6 pounds of milk would feed twin kids, so that is the figure I used. It takes a huge amount of energy to produce milk, and if the doe is not getting that energy, along with the protein she needs from her diet, she will pull it out of her body, or reduce her milk yield. For these reasons, I would recommend adding a high protein pellet to your milking doe's diet along with her grain ration.

	DM (lbs)	TDN (g)	TCP (g)	% TCP	Ca (g)	P (g)
110 lb (50 kg) Doe – Lactating	4.8 lbs	1833g	326g	14.9%	13g	9.1g
176 lb (80 kg) Doe -Lactating	5 lbs	2169g	372g	14.9%	15g	10.5g

Growing kid: Again, these rations are very hard to standardize. Different kids grow at different rates. I have used a 66 pound kid growing at a rate of .5 pounds a day, because that is my goal for my meat kids.   Many times this rate of gain fluctuates between .25 and .65 pounds a day.   In addition, if the kid is still nursing, he is receiving a large amount of his nutrients through his mother's milk. I find that I can hit the ration requirements that I want by adding a high protein 'milk pellet' to the my kids' diet. One problem that you might run into, is the size of the pellet. Kids need about a ¼ inch or 3/8 inch pellet. Also, kids will not get the nutrition they need if they are not able to go into a creep and eat free choice.

It would be impossible for me to guess at the size of your kids, the size that they stop drinking milk, and the rate of gain that you are aiming for.   However, let me give you some basic body weights, with the same rate of gain figured in, so you can try to make informed judgements about the nutrient requirements of your kids.

	DM (lbs)	TDN (g)	TCP (g)	% TCP	Ca (g)	P (g)
22 lb (10 kg) Kid + .5 lb / day	2 lbs	639	89g	9.5%	4g	2.8g
44 lb (20 kg) Kid + .5 lb / day	2.65 lbs	800	111g	9.5%	5g	3.5g
66 lb (30 kg) Kid + .5 lb / day	3 lbs	943g	130g	9.5%	6g	4.2g

Figuring a Feed Ration

At the end of this chapter, I will give you a nutritional table for as many different feeds as possible. Your job is to figure out what your goats are eating, and what is missing from their ration.

If you have goats on pasture, you should figure out what is in the pasture, how much dry matter is in the feed, then compare what the goats are eating to the above tables. Maybe your goats are doing great. They are sleek, healthy, growing and you are totally happy with weight gains and birth weights. I would say you are doing something right! If you are not as perfectly happy with all these things as you might be, I am handing you a tool.

If you feed your goats a ration, it is relatively easy to find out if it is appropriate for their needs. Let's say you feed 4 pounds of alfalfa hay and 1 pound of a corn and barley mix. Let's look at the values from the table at the back of this chapter:

The following data is 'as fed':

	Lbs feed	DM (lbs)	TDN (g/lb)	TCP (g)	%TCP	Ca (g)	P(g)
Alfalfa hay, early bloom	1	.90	245	73.55	16.20	5.76	0.90
Corn	1	.87	352	43.05	9.48	0.20	1.15
Barley	1	.88	336	53.94	11.88	0.20	1.52

15

I have given you all the actual nutritional amounts that would be found in the feed on an 'as fed' basis. In other words, in one pound of alfalfa, there is actually .9 pounds of dry food and the nutrients listed are actually in that .9 pounds, you don't have to calculate out the water.

Now, take the nutrients above and multiply them times the amount you are going to be feeding. For example, all the nutrients for alfalfa would be times 4 pounds, so the first section of your feed ration worksheet would now look like this:

Feed Ration Worksheet

Type of feed	Lbs feed	DM (lbs)	TDN (g/lb)	TCP (g)	% TCP	Ca (g)	P(g)
Feed #1 copy values:	B.	C.	D.	E.	F.	G.	H.
Alfalfa hay, early bloom	1	.90	245	73.5	16.2	5.7	0.9
In space "J", write the pounds of Feed #1 to be fed per day, per animal:	J. 4						
ROW 1	Multiply B – H times J. and write those values here: K 4	L. 3.6	M. 980	N. 294	P. 64.8	Q. 22.8	R. 3.6

Now wait. Let's just pause for a moment. If I lose you here, you'll be lost for good. Do you see what I did? I filled in the values for alfalfa, from the table at the end of this chapter, on the first line. Then I decided how much alfalfa I was going to feed each goat per day, and filled it in on space J. Then I multiplied that number times each of the values on the first line, and put that total on the bottom line. Now I know what the total nutritional value is for the alfalfa part of my feed ration. (Don't get excited about the %TCP column, because we are going to average this column when we get all done.)

Now, let's do the same thing for ½ pound of corn per goat, per day:

Feed Ration Worksheet

Type of feed	Lbs feed	DM (lbs)	TDN (g/lb)	TCP (g)	% TCP	Ca (g)	P(g)
Feed #2 copy values:	S.	T.	U.	V.	W.	X.	Y.
Corn	1	.87	352	43.1	9.48	0.2	1.15
In space "Z", write the pounds of Feed #1 to be fed per day, per animal:	Z. .5						
ROW 2	Multiply S-Y times Z. and write those values here: aa. .5	bb. .44	cc. 176	dd. 21.5	ee. 4.74	ff. .10	gg. .58

Now we know the nutritional value in ½ pound of corn. Let's do it again for barley:

Feed Ration Worksheet

Type of feed	Lbs feed	DM (lbs)	TDN (g/lb)	TCP (g)	% TCP	Ca (g)	P(g)
Feed #3 copy values: Barley	hh. 1	ii. .88	jj. 336	kk. 53.9	ll. 11.9	mm. 0.2	nn. 1.52
In space "pp", write the pounds of Feed #1 to be fed per day, per animal:	pp. .5						
ROW 3 — Multiply hh-nn times pp. and write those values here:	qq. .5	rr. .11	ss. 168	tt. 26.9	uu. 5.95	vv. .10	ww. .76

We have now figured the nutritional values for each of the components of our feed ration: 4 lbs. alfalfa, ½ lb. corn, and ½ lb. barley. We need to know how they add up when we feed them together. So we are going to stack the tables on top of each other, and add each of the total rows (marked by a ►) to get a grand total: ★

Feed Ration Worksheet

Type of feed	Lbs feed	DM (lbs)	TDN (g/lb)	TCP (g)	% TCP	Ca (g)	P(g)
Feed #1 copy values:	B.	C.	D.	E.	F.	G.	H.
Alfalfa hay, early bloom	1	.90	245	73.5	16.2	5.7	0.90
In space "J", write the pounds of Feed #1 to be fed per day, per animal:	J. 4						
ROW 1 — Multiply B – H times J. and write those values here:	K. 4	L. 3.6	M. 980	N. 294	P. 64.8	Q. 22.8	R. 3.6
Feed #2 copy values:	S.	T.	U.	V.	W.	X.	Y.
Corn	1	.87	352	43.1	9.48	0.2	1.15
In space "Z", write the pounds of Feed #1 to be fed per day, per animal:	Z. .5						
ROW 2 — Multiply S-Y times Z. and write those values here:	aa. .5	bb. .44	cc. 176	dd. 21.5	ee. 4.74	ff. .10	gg. .58
Feed #3 copy values:	hh.	ii.	jj.	kk.	ll.	mm.	nn.
Barley	1	.88	336	53.9	11.9	0.2	1.52
In space "pp", write the pounds of Feed #1 to be fed per day, per animal:	pp. .5						
ROW 3 — Multiply hh-nn times pp. and write those values here:	qq. .5	rr. .44	ss. 168	tt. 26.9	uu. 5.95	vv. .10	ww. .76
Total Row 4 — Add all values for ROWs 1,2 and 3 and enter those values here:	zz. 5.0	4.5	1324	342	xx. 75.5	23	4.94

OK. These are our nutritional values for our complete ration. It is almost time to compare them to the chart for the requirements of our goat, but we have a serious problem with the %TCP column. We can't possibly have 75.5% protein. We have to average this number by the total pounds that we fed. So, I guess I will have to add a line to the worksheet to do this average:

In this space, find the average %TCP by dividing the total %TCP figure in space xx by the total number of pounds fed (in space zz). Enter the resulting figure here:	yy. 15.1	

Now, I would feel better if I saw all the totals lined up together. So I think we should bring the totals down from our total line, but change the %TCP to the 15.1% figure we got when we averaged. The last three lines of our worksheet would then look like this:

Type of feed		Lbs feed	DM (lbs)	TDN (g/lb)	TCP (g)	% TCP	Ca (g)	P(g)
Total **Row 4**	Add all values for ROWs 1,2 and 3 and enter those values here:	zz. 5	4.48	1324	342	xx. 75.5	23	4.9
In this space, find the average %TCP by dividing the total %TCP figure in space xx by the total number of pounds fed (in space zz). Enter the resulting figure here:						yy. 15.1		
Bring down all values from ROW 4, except use 'yy' for %TCP. TOTAL!		5	4.48	1324	342	yy. 15.1	23	4.9

Now let's compare this ration to the nutritional needs of a 110 pound doe in late pregnancy:

	DM (lbs)	TDN (g)	TCP (g)	%TCP	Ca (g)	P (g)
110 lb (50 kg) Doe in late Pregnancy	4 lbs	1192g	192g	10.8%	6g	4.2g

That actually looks pretty good. A little high in protein and calcium, but those are two areas that are OK to be high in. This is all assuming, of course, that she eats all of her 4 pounds of alfalfa, instead of throwing it around or sleeping on it. And it is assuming that you have bought some good 18% protein alfalfa.

Now, just to play devil's advocate, let's say that this doe is out on a pasture that is made up mostly of good orchard grass.

The following data is 'as fed':

	Lbs feed	DM (lbs)	TDN (g/lb)	TCP (g)	% TCP	Ca (g)	P(g)
Orchard grass, fresh early	1 lb	.25 lb	75	13.39	2.95%	0.28	0.44
Corn	1	.87 lb	352	43.05	9.5%	.20	1.15
Barley	1	.88 lb	335	53.93	11.9%	.20	1.52

15

How many pounds of grass would the same pregnant doe have to eat, along with the same grain ration to get enough nutrition? Let's get out a fresh worksheet, and plug in the numbers. Please do it with me so you will get used to using the worksheet.

Feed Ration Worksheet

Type of feed	Lbs feed	DM lbs	TDN (g/lb)	TCP (g)	% TCP	Ca (g)	P(g)
Feed #1 copy values: Orchard grass, fresh early	B. 1 lb	C. .25	D. 75	E. 13.4	F. 2.95	G. .28	H. .44
In space "J", write the pounds of Feed #1 to be fed per day, per animal:	J. 11.5						
ROW 1 Multiply B – H times J. and write those values here:	K. 11.5	L. 2.8	M. 863	N. 154	P. 33.9	Q. 3.2	R. 5.0
Feed #2 copy values: Corn	S. 1 lb	T. .87	U. 352	V. 43.1	W. 9.48	X. 0.2	Y. 1.15
In space "Z", write the pounds of Feed #1 to be fed per day, per animal:	Z. .5						
ROW 2 Multiply S-Y times Z. and write those values here:	aa. .5	bb. .44	cc. 176	dd. 21.5	ee. 4.74	ff. .10	gg. .58

Feed #3 copy values:		hh.	ii.	jj.	kk.	ll.	mm.	nn.
Barley		1 lb	.88	336	53.9	11.9	0.20	1.52
In space "pp", write the pounds of Feed #1 to be fed per day, per animal:		pp. .5						
ROW 3	Multiply hh-nn times pp. and write those values here:	qq. .5	rr. .44	ss. 168	tt. 26.9	uu. 5.95	vv. .10	ww. .76
Total Row 4	Add all values for ROWs 1,2 and 3 and enter those values	zz. 12.5	3.7	1207	202	xx. 44.5	3.4	6.4
In this space, find the average %TCP by dividing the total %TCP figure in space xx by the total number of pounds fed (in space zz). Enter the resulting figure here:						yy. 3.56		
Bring down all values from ROW 4, except use 'yy' for %TCP. TOTAL!		12.5	3.8	1207	202	yy. 3.56	3.4	6.4

	DM (lbs)	TDN (g)	TCP (g)	%TCP	Ca (g)	P (g)
110 lb (50 kg) Doe in late Pregnancy	4 lbs	1192g	192g	10.8 %	6g	4.2g

To get enough dry matter, TDN, TCP and phosphorus, this doe has to eat 12.5 pounds of feed. There is nothing wrong with eating twelve and a half pounds of grass a day to get 3.75 pounds of dry feed, but she is going to have to spend some serious time at it, have a very good rumen capacity, and make a lot of trips to the little girl's room. There is also a question of the energy that it will take her to digest that amount of feed. If there is not enough energy in the feed to digest it, then it just won't get digested, and you will have a sick goat. That is why you can't effectively feed an animal straw or a lot of dry, sun bleached weeds. There is not enough energy in the feed to do anything with it.

Back to our pregnant doe. Her protein shows low in percentage but good in grams, this is because of all that water. If she really digested 12 pounds of grass, then she did meet her protein requirement, even if the percentage shows low. She will need a calcium supplement, however, probably in the form of loose minerals.

On the next page, I have given you a blank feed ration worksheet. Please feel free to copy this worksheet, and enlarge it if you need to, to assist you in figuring your feeds. If you can learn to use this worksheet, you should be able to figure out the approximate nutritional content of any feed ration, if you have the nutritional contents of each of the ingredients in the ration.

What about Pelletized Feeds?

Pelletized feeds can be produced to meet the exact nutritional needs of your goats.   There is probably a company right there in your town who would do it. But goats cannot live on pellets alone.   Their rumens must have long fibers to keep working. So, even if you are able to get some good pellets, be sure to feed at least 1 to 2 pounds a day per goat of long fiber hay.

The biggest problem with a pelletized mix tends to be the expense. However, if the hay type feed that you normally feed, is very prone to waste, like alfalfa is, you should carefully consider the effect of waste on your feed bill. As you will see in the next section, I have carefully evaluated the cost of wasted feed on my ranch, and decided there was a way to use pellets with reduced waste, in spite of the cost.

What this means is, if you are paying $200 a ton for a complete mix, your money is better spent than if you spend $100 a ton on poor quality hay.   My nutritionist explained to me that I should be looking at the "cost of the nutrients", rather than the overall cost of the feed.   For instance, if a high protein supplement costs $100 a ton, and you need to feed ¼ pound per day, your protein is costing you 1.25 cents per day.   If you are feeding a different protein supplement that only costs you $50 per ton, but you need to feed 1 pound a day to get the same

Feed Ration Worksheet

Type of feed	Lbs feed	DM (lbs)	TDN (g/lb)	TCP (g)	% TCP	Ca (g)	P(g)
Feed #1 copy values:	B. 1 lb	C.	D.	E.	F.	G.	H.
In space "J", write the pounds of Feed #1 to be fed per day, per animal:	J.						
ROW 1 — Multiply B – H times J. and write those values here:	K.	L.	M.	N.	P.	Q.	R.
Feed #2 copy values:	S. 1 lb	T.	U.	V.	W.	X.	Y.
In space 'Z' write the pounds of Feed #2 to be fed per day, per animal:	Z.						
ROW 2 — Multiply S-Y times Z and write those values here:	aa.	bb.	cc.	dd.	ee.	ff.	gg.
Feed #3 copy values:	hh. 1 lb	ii.	jj.	kk.	ll.	mm.	nn.
In space 'pp' write the pounds of Feed #2 to be fed per day, per animal:	pp.						
ROW 3 — Multiply hh-nn times pp and write those values here:	qq.	rr.	ss.	tt.	uu.	vv.	ww.
Total Row 4 — Add all values for ROWs 1,2 and 3 and enter those values:	zz.				xx.		
In this space, find the average %TCP by dividing the total %TCP figure in space xx by the total number of pounds fed (in space zz). Enter the resulting figure here:					yy.		
Bring down all values from ROW 4, except use 'yy' for %TCP. TOTAL!					yy.		

nutrition, your protein is costing you 2.5 cents per day. Even though the initial cost of the feed is lower.

A note: Toxoplasmosis can be spread if your cats use your pelletized feed for kitty litter. If you decide to use pelletized feed, keep it covered.

Automatic Feeding

Many people say that you cannot put your goats on automatic feeders because goats are such pigs. This is just not true. Yes, goats are pigs, but one of the main reasons that they are pigs, is our insistence on feeding them in pens. When goats are fed in pens, twice a day, they have a limited amount of feed in front of them, and the temptation to hoard it becomes paramount. However, I have had my goats on free, constant availability, feed for over a year.

I have found that when feed is always available, in an unlimited supply, they revert to their natural instincts. Goats are browsers. They naturally eat one bite of this and one bite of that. They do not naturally gorge on one feed. When they are being free fed, they do not guard the feed, so all the goats get as much as they want to eat. When the feed is always there, and they know it will always be there, the goats develop a different pattern of eating. My goats go 'out' to the bulk feeders five times a day. When they get there, the dominant goats eat first. Then they work through the chain of command, until even the weakest goats get to eat as much as they want. They just wait until last. That's OK, because the feed isn't going anywhere and there is plenty of time. No one is frantic, they don't fight, and my smaller goats look as good as the bigger goats. However, if your goats are in a pen, I doubt that free feeding would work.

Let me just tell you what I do. I am not an expert on this subject, and I have not found any studies. Then, you can use my experience to make a reasonable conclusion about what you might want to try. I have about 50 does who are all out together on 20 acres. The 20 acres consists of 5 acres of pasture, and 15 acres of sagebrush and naturally occurring grasses. I have two bulk feeders that are about 600 feet from the end of the pasture where the barn is (I'll call this end, the end by the barn, the top of the pasture). The goats walk out to the bulk feeders five times a day. Then they wander off into the sagebrush to browse, and then they come back to the top of the pasture for a nap. Five times a day. The last trip in the evening, they come and lay by their goat houses and waterers, which are here at the top of the pasture, outside my bedroom window. (Notice that I say that they lay 'by' their goat houses. My goats don't actually go into their houses unless the temperatures are under about 10 degrees F, or there is moisture falling out of the sky.)

I like this routine, because it allows me to check on my goats five times a day, just by looking out the window. I can even sit by the window and watch them interact, walk around, and rest. For one thing, I like watching, and interacting with, my goats. For another thing, this routine allows me to make sure no one is sick or needs attention.

What is in my bulk feeders, you ask? Well, I do buy that expensive pelletized feed. I have it made to be a complete ration for my goats, and expect them to eat about three pounds of it a day, each. You would be surprised how nearly this works out, even if they are feeding themselves. I have the pellets in a 2 ton round pig feeder, and the feed company just comes and fills it, with a truck with an auger on it, once a month. They don't even ask, they just show up, and many times I don't even know they have been here until I find an invoice stuck on my car.

In the other bulk feeder, I put alfalfa/grass hay. This feeder is one of those 16 foot calf feeders with a hay rack over a rubber trough. I only feed about two bales a week of hay. The hay is just to be sure that they are eating enough long fiber to keep their rumens working.

I don't have to feed from about June 1st until mid October, because the goats are out on an area of lush vegetation. My pasture is an alfalfa, grass, weeds mixture, and the sagebrush has a lot of natural grass, and rye grass in it. I do give some supplemental feed to any does that are still raising kids in the summer, and I <u>always</u> creep feed my kids.

Now that I have told you my secrets, let me tell you why I feed that way. I have a very small work force, and what I do have is threatening to go off to college soon. I love raising goats, but don't have the temperament to raise very many, so I raise a few good breeding stock animals. I have been trying to find a way to feed my animals without spending as much time at it everyday, for years. I was also very frustrated with the amount of alfalfa hay that the goats wasted. When I used to feed my goats in pens, and even now for my bucks, I had to clean out the feeders every week. There is just so much that the goats walk on or potty on, or that gets wet or compressed, and the goats won't eat it. With bulk feeding, they eat every bit of the pellets, and clean up the hay that I put out. Plus, they are walking long distances, which is very good for them. They don't fight. And I don't have to stress getting the right combinations of personalities together to be sure everyone will get enough to eat.

In the past, I found that I was having to feed 6 pounds of hay, plus 1 lb. of grain supplement, to get enough nutrition into my goats, because they wasted so much of it. So the actual real life costs for the feed I was feeding when my goats were in pens was:

> 6lbs X 50 goats = 300 lbs. per day
> 300 lbs. X 365 days = 109,500 lbs. per year
> 109,500 divided by 2000 = 54.75 tons per year
> 54.75 tons X $80.00 = $4,380 for hay
> + 1 lb. grain per goat X 50 goats = 50 lbs. per day
> = 18,250lbs grain per year
> divided by 50 lb. bags = 365 bags
> 365 bags X $5.50 per bag = $2,007 for grain
> $2,007 for grain + $4380 for hay = $6387.50

Now I feed bulk feeds for 8 months of the year, plus some supplemental pellets during the rest of the year for the does with kids, and creep feed for the kids (I fed this anyway). My current costs are:

> 3lbs X 50 goats = 150 lbs. pellets
> 150 lbs. X 240 days = 57,600 lbs.
> 57,600 lbs. divided by 2000 = 28.8 tons

28.8 tons + 1 ton supplemental pellets = 30 tons

30 tons of pellets X $200 = $6,000 TOTAL

I barter for my hay, and I don't have to get too excited about the quality, because it isn't the main nutrition source.

My costs are about the same, there is no waste, and I don't have to feed every day. It works for me. By the way, I have pretty nice goats, and they tend to be in good condition. However, no system is perfect. I have one older Boer doe who definitely over-eats. I have to wonder if more Boers will over-eat as they get older, although so far they haven't. I don't have the smaller ones standing around being hungry, though. Like I said, it works for me. I have no idea if it would work for you.

Changing Feeds

A goat's rumen develops the bacteria and microbes necessary to break down the feed that the goat is accustomed to eating. When you introduce a new feed, the rumen needs time to develop a whole new set of bacteria. So always start any new feed slowly. Lets say you bought a goat from another state. The breeder gave you a bag of the feed that the goat was used to. When you get the goat home, make her comfortable in her new pen and feed her the feed you brought home from the breeder. The next day, mix 2/3 of her old food and 1/3 the feed you are going to be giving her. The second day give her 1/2 and 1/2. The third day give her 2/3 of the new food and 1/3 of the old. By the forth day her rumen will be adjusted and you shouldn't have to worry.

Never give a goat a lot of something new, even if they are eating their normal ration too. Especially grains. If a goat is not used to a grain feed, and does not have the preexisting bacteria and microbes to properly digest it, it can sit in the goat's intestinal tract and ferment. This causes Enterotoxemia, and the goat can die. Please read about Enterotoxemia in the "Health Needs and Potential Problems" chapter of this book.

Vitamins and Minerals

Most of the vitamins and minerals your goat needs will be supplied by their feed. Vitamin and mineral supplements can be purchased in many different forms. It is always a good idea to have a mineral block or loose mineral supplement out for your goats in case they need it. I believe in free choice mineral supplements. If you have several things out that have different ingredients in them, the goats can choose what they need.

Never put out a supplement without first carefully checking the contents. You should always have salt available to your goats, especially in hot weather. Goats are not as sensitive to copper as sheep are, but they can not take as much as cattle and horses. Selenium is an important mineral that is missing from many soils across the country. Calcium is a very important mineral, as are zinc and phosphorus. Iodine is also very important to prevent gout.

Vitamins A and D are extremely important to milk production and animal health. Vitamin A deficiencies can affect vision, while Vitamin D deficiencies affect the animal's ability to absorb and utilize calcium and phosphorus.

It is always a good idea to talk to your veterinarian about the minerals that are important to feed in your area. In addition, a local animal nutritionist may be able to make you aware of the vitamins and mineral supplementation necessary in your area.

Poisonous Plants

It is unusual for goats to become poisoned by eating hazardous plants, because goats are browsers; they eat a bite of this and then a bite of that. If something bothers them, they normally just don't go back to it. However, if a goat is hungry, or inexperienced, it can poison itself by being a glutton.

Here is a list of plants that are poisonous to a greater or lesser extent. It would be a good idea to avoid them all.

<u>Hazardous Plants:</u>

Aconite	Alder
Arum	Azaleas
Anemone	Bracken
Beet Leaves	Black Nightshade
Broom	Butterbur
Buttercup	Buckthorn
Box	Byrony
Celandine	Charlock
Cupresses	Daffodil
Dogs Mercury	Deadly Nightshade
Ergot	Foxglove
Fools Parsley	Fungi
Ground Ivy	Gladiolus
Gourds	Hellebores
Hemlock	Holm Oak
Horsetail	Iris
Juniper	Knotgrass
Knotweed	Kingcup
Laburnum	Locoweed
Lords and Ladies	Lilac
Lupins (yellow)	Marsh Mallow
Mangold Leaves	Milkweed
Mountain Laurel	Mulleins
Nightshades (all)	Old Mans Beard
Poppy	Pennycress
Privet	Potato Tops
Pines	Ragwort
Rhododendron	Rhubarb Leaves
Rush	Spindle berry, branch & Lvs
Spurge Laurel	Thorn Apple
Tansy	Tomato Greenstuff
Tormentil	Waterdrop Wort
Yellow Flag	Wild Cherry, wilted
Yew	

Composition of Goat Feeds

National Research Council Composition of Goat Feeds[15] Feed	Actual nutritional values in one pound of feed. (As fed basis) DM (lb)	TDN (g/lb)	TCP (g/lb)	% TCP	Ca (g/lb)	P (g/lb)
Alfalfa meal for pellets	.92	255	79.36	17.48	6.65	1.04
Alfalfa hay- dry full bloom	.90	225	61.29	13.50	5.11	0.90
Alfalfa hay- early bloom	.90	245	73.55	16.20	5.76	0.90
Alfalfa, fresh	.24	60	21.47	4.73	2.14	0.33
Barley grain	.88	336	53.94	11.88	0.20	1.52
Barley, fresh	.21	60	19.45	4.28	0.57	0.38
Bermudagrass, fresh	.34	93	18.52	4.08	0.82	0.32
Brome hay mature	.93	220	24.49	5.39	NA	NA
Brome, smooth hay early	.91	231	49.99	11.01	1.12	0.83
Buffalograss, fresh	.72	177	19.29	4.25	NA	NA
Cabbage, fresh	.09	34	8.42	1.85	NA	NA
Canary grass, fresh reed	.27	80	14.22	3.13	0.50	0.43
Canary grass, reed hay	.91	227	42.55	9.37	1.57	1.03
Carrot, root, fresh	.12	46	5.39	1.19	0.22	0.19
Chickpea seeds	.91	314	89.65	19.75	0.70	1.53
Clover, red hay	.89	222	64.65	14.24	6.18	1.01
Corn grain	.87	352	43.05	9.48	0.20	1.15
Cotton Seed Meal	.91	314	186.74	41.13	0.74	4.63
Cowpea, fresh	.15	44	11.03	2.43	1.30	0.19
Dallis-grass, fresh early	.26	74	27.39	6.03	0.77	0.50
Kudzu hay	.91	227	59.08	13.01	9.71	1.45
Lettuce, fresh	.05	16	4.99	1.10	0.20	0.10
Milkvetch, Nuttall fresh	.28	80	18.81	4.14	NA	0.23
Millet, fresh	.22	63	27.07	5.96	NA	NA
Molasses	.78	280	30.10	6.63	0.60	0.11
Oak, live, fresh leaves	.50	104	23.15	5.10	NA	0.25
Oat hay	.91	252	38.42	8.46	0.99	0.91
Oats	.89	311	53.74	11.84	0.28	1.54
Oats, fresh	.20	56	12.35	2.72	0.25	1.53
Onion, bulb fresh	.10	0	4.59	1.01	0.00	0.18
Orchard grass, fresh early	.25	75	13.39	2.95	0.28	0.44
Pea Pods, garden fresh	.18	57	12.09	2.66	NA	NA
Peanut hay	.91	227	44.62	9.83	5.08	0.62

Feed	DM (lb)	TDN (g/lb)	TCP (g/lb)	% TCP	Ca (g/lb)	P (g/lb)
Peanut kernels	.94	363	187.9	41.4	1.18	2.81
Potato, tubers	.23	85	9.92	2.19	0.04	0.25
Ragweed fresh, early	.27	82	20.47	4.51	2.06	0.20
Rape seeds meal	.91	285	167.73	36.95	2.77	4.30
Rape, turnip fresh	.15	39	5.99	1.32	NA	NA
Red-top hay full bloom	.91	231	38.84	8.55	NA	NA
Redtop, fresh midbloom	.39	110	13.10	2.89	0.58	0.41
Rice grain	.89	323	36.37	8.01	0.28	1.21
Rye grain	.88	336	55.13	12.14	0.28	1.48
Rye, fresh	.24	75	17.32	3.82	0.42	0.36
Ryegrass, fresh	.24	66	11.11	2.45	NA	NA
Safflower hay	.85	262	49.40	10.88	5.40	1.58
Safflower seeds meal	.92	305	195.89	43.15	1.59	5.85
Safflower, fresh	.15	39	10.83	2.39	0.75	0.26
Safflower, leaves fresh	.16	45	20.99	4.62	1.23	0.33
Sagebrush, early	.29	87	16.06	3.54	0.63	0.16
Sesame seeds meal	.93	325	207.31	45.66	9.16	6.16
Sorghum, fresh	.35	105	6.36	1.40	NA	NA
Soybean hay, mature	.90	184	58.84	12.96	4.25	1.14
Soybean hay, midbloom	.94	226	75.96	16.73	5.38	1.15
Soybean seeds, meal	.90	360	203.89	44.91	1.39	2.86
Sudangrass hay, early	.90	237	63.74	14.04	3.15	1.47
Sudangrass hay, late	.88	228	55.53	12.23	1.72	1.20
Sudangrass, fresh early	.18	57	13.73	3.02	0.35	0.34
Sudangrass, fresh midbloom	.23	66	9.19	2.02	0.45	0.38
Sunflower seed meal	.93	274	210.27	46.31	1.86	4.14
Sweet potato tubers	.33	121	7.49	1.65	0.15	0.22
Timothy hay, full bloom	.89	234	30.71	6.76	1.74	0.81
Timothy hay, late vegetative	.89	259	47.28	10.41	2.67	1.37
Trefoil, birdsfoot hay	.91	260	59.91	13.20	NA	NA
Trefoil, fresh	.15	44	11.92	2.63	NA	NA
Wheat grain	.89	356	64.65	14.24	0.16	1.70

Note: To convert the above numbers to % grams per kilogram, divide by 4.54 (except the %TCP which would remain the same).

NOTES:

Breeding

Breeding is the beginning of production. You can't produce the kids you need to make a profit, if you don't get your does bred. I talked in Chapter 4 about buying your bucks and does for breeding and the many different things that go into that purchase. Now, you have only to get the bucks and does together in a socially acceptable situation. What is socially acceptable to a goat? Why, everything, of course! But *you* will want to have a plan.

The Smell of a Good Buck

As a rule of thumb, bucks begin to come into rut (and can be bred) at about 5 ½ months old. I hear all the time about the little buck who bred his sister at 4 months old, but that seems to be the exception rather than the rule. Still, it is a good reason to wean your bucks at 3 months old, and move them away from the girls. I have also found that a 5 ½ month old buckling may not get every doe he is presented with pregnant until the next heat. So you must be careful of your expectations for a young buck in his first breeding year. His sperm count will not be as high as it will be in a year or so, and he can not cover as many

does at one time. If you are using a very young buck
(under one year old) you should put his does in with him,
one at a time, as they come into heat, then take them out
once he has bred them one or two times. This will reserve
his resources for more breeding.

**Picture 21: . You can't produce the kids you need to make a
profit, if you don't get your does bred.** *

When you put a doe in heat in with your buck, he will
mount her several times, but not seem to get much
accomplished. You will know when he has actually bred
her because he will throw back his head and *fall off* to one
side, and the doe will tuck her tail under and kind of
hunch up. The buck will then rest for a few minutes and
then breed her again. Once is generally enough, but I like
to give him twice, just to be sure.

Bucks produce a musk smell when they are in rut through
the glands behind their horns. They also add a lovely
cologne by spraying their front legs and faces (and
anything else they can reach) liberally with urine. The
resulting aroma is truly delightful – if you are a doe. To

---

* This picture donated by Kids-R-Us Goat Farm from Uvalde, Texas.

humans, it is slightly less attractive. An interesting note: the smell of a buck in rut is usually far more offensive to women than to men. And if you get it on your hands, gloves, clothes, or house it stays there until it is thoroughly scrubbed off. Some people maintain that you can go to your neighbor's buck, rub a rag all over his head, put the rag in a jar and take it home to your does. They are supposed to respond to this rag with tail wagging and general female silliness. If you don't have a buck, you are welcome to try it. However, in my experience, the only true aphrodisiac for a doe is a real live buck.

A Buck tip: If your buck starts to get aggressive with you, carry a spray bottle filled with vinegar whenever you go into his pen. Vinegar sprayed into his face occasionally will not injure his eyes, but it will make him shy of spray bottles.

Breeding out of Season

Goats normally breed September through January. That way they will kid in February through June. If you think about it, God was pretty smart to set it up that way, because baby goats do better when they are born in cooler weather. No, really, that is a fact. Most old time goat breeders contend that kids born in cooler weather are stronger because they have fewer bacteria and worms to attack their system until they are up and running.

Regardless of the reasoning behind it, there are several factors that work together to make goats breed in the fall. One of these is light. When the length of the day starts to shorten, the breeding system in a goat switches on. Does come into heat and bucks come into rut.

Another, and apparently stronger factor is heat. The does do not want to cycle, and many bucks are not fertile, when the climate is too hot. The heat kills off enough of the buck's sperm to lower their count, making them infertile.

Many meat goat raisers are very interested in disrupting the grand plan, and breeding on a year-around basis so that they can get three kid crops within 2 years time. The biggest obstacle to this plan does not seem to be the light issue. It is finding a buck that is fertile during the warmer months.

However, the breeds of goats that are coming into the country from overseas are changing that whole cycle. These animals have been bred in opposite light and heat conditions. Both the Boer and the Kiko have been bred to produce in high multiples regardless of the climatic conditions. So, in most areas, meat goats will breed all year around. In my area, the Northwestern United States, you can kid in virtually any month of the year if you just put your buck out with your does about a month after the does kid. They will often rebreed at 40 to 100 days after they have kidded. This pertains to dairy does, as well as meat does. The does seem to cycle if the buck is in rut.

However, the buck isn't as aromatic in the spring and summer as he is in the fall. If you put your meat buck out with your does in the spring and summer, he will probably come back into rut, but not quite as strongly. You may get a much lower pregnancy rate than you would if you put him out in the fall, but you will probably have some pregnancies. In addition, not all bucks, not even meat bucks, will be fertile in the off season. I have owned one Boer buck that was only fertile in the fall, and then only when the weather cooled down. But I have owned several that bred right through the summer.

Some other factors to consider if you are wanting to breed out of season: If your does are on a base ration of hay and water, then are switched to a production ration with more grain, they may cycle. If your does are weaning their kids, they usually cycle three weeks after the kids are completely removed. If a does is penned up with a buck in rut, she will often cycle in 7 days.

When is a Doe in Heat?

As I stated in the last section, does tend to cycle in the fall, after about September first. A young doeling will begin to come into heat at about 4 months old. A normal heat cycle is 21 days, but the actual range is more like 18 to 25 days. The doe will remain in heat for 12 to 36 hours. Sometimes a doe will come into heat, breed, and then come into heat again in 7 to 10 days. She will usually get pregnant the second time. This is a normal, and relatively common occurrence, especially at the beginning of the breeding season. I have a doe who does this every single year. She always conceives triplets on the second breeding, but she will then re-breed, just for practice, every month for the rest of the season.

Most does will tell you when they are in heat. They will stand by the fence nearest to the buck, wag their tails, stare at him, and cry. However, as in all species, every doe is different. Some stand there and scream. Some stand by the fence and wag their tails like crazy. Some does have a large amount of vaginal discharge when they are in heat. Some butt heads and mount, or are mounted by, other does. Usually, it is the doe that is standing to be mounted by the other does that is the one in heat, but this is not cut and dry either.

If you go out to a doe that you think is in heat, and push down on her rump, just above the tail head, and she stands still, or even wags her tail, you know she is in heat. (A doe that is not in heat will tuck her hips under.) This is called, imaginatively enough, 'standing heat'. Some does do not say a word when they are in heat, and the only way to catch them is to put them in with the buck and let him figure it out on his own.

When to Breed

One of the most frequently asked questions is, "When do I breed my does?" First of all, the doe must be big enough to breed. This means <u>at least</u> 70 to 80 pounds, and over 7 months old. I like to wait until my does are 9 months, but this is not always practical if you are trying to stick to a schedule.

Next, you need to decide when you want to kid. I know, you just want to breed your does, but the result is going to be little kids hitting the ground all over your ranch, and you need to be ready for them.

When to kid is a more complicated question than most people realize. The gestation period for a goat is 145 to 155 days, so figure 150 days, or 5 months. You need to take several things into consideration:

♥ What will the weather be like in my area when it is time for these kids to be born?

♥ How many goats can I comfortably kid out at one time?

♥ What other commitments will be going on in my life at that time of year?   What about planting, taxes, children, travel, goat shows, etc.

♥ If I'm going to give shots on a monthly schedule, how can I arrange these kiddings to reduce my work load?

♥ How many times do I want to disrupt my life to kid out my goats?   Should I group these kiddings more, or spread them out?

In my area, it is best to breed the goats the first week of September to kid out in the first week of February. Why? Because, in the valley I live in, we always get Indian summer the second and third week of February. So the kids can get up and going, and be about three weeks old, before the cold weather hits again. It is too cold to kid the end of February and March, so I try to group the rest of my breeding in the month of November to kid in April.

This schedule means that my February kids will be 9 months old when I want to breed them in November, but my April kids will only be 7 months old. But if I wait to breed those April kids until January, then their kids will be born in June and too young to breed at all the next fall. Then I will have to make a decision based on schedules and the weight of my does that will affect how I breed the *next* year.

How to Manage Breeding

There are several ways to manage your breeding. One option is pasture breeding. This is probably the most common way to get the job done in a meat herd. To pasture breed you just put the buck out with the does during the month that you want them bred, and expect that he will get the job done. He generally does. However, unless you put a marking harness on him (this is a harness, built for sheep, that holds a crayon between a buck's front legs, so that when he mounts a doe it leaves a mark on her rump), you will not know when, or if, your does are bred for sure. Sometimes, especially with younger bucks, a buck in a pasture breeding situation will expend all his resources on one doe by breeding her over and over. Then, when another doe comes into heat, he doesn't have anything left for her. That is why it is a good idea to leave your does in with a buck, if you are pasture breeding, for over 40 days (long enough for at least two heat cycles). This gives the buck another shot if he missed one the first time around.

Another option is called 'hand breeding'. In this method, you put your buck in a sturdy pen next to the does. Putting a buck that has not been near the does before, into close contact with your does may stimulate them to come into heat. When a doe is standing at the fence wagging her tail and kissing on the buck, even though the rest of the herd has gone out to eat, she is in heat. Put her into his pen, let him breed her twice, then remove her. This works very well if you have people around to watch and be sure you catch the does as they come into heat, and if your does come into obvious heat.

My favorite breeding plan is a combination of the above options. I like to move the buck into a pen right next to the does at the first of the month in which I want them to be bred. Then, I hand breed any doe that comes into heat in the first two weeks of the month. Any remaining does that are scheduled to be bred in that month, that have not been hand bred by the second week, are then put into his pen. The marking harness is put on the buck. When I see a doe has been marked, I pull her out of the pen. This gives me nearly exact breeding dates on most of my does and keeps them on my schedule.

How do I decide who to breed in which month? Again, it has to do with age and size. I breed in September and November. My does that are over one year old are bred in September, and my does that are under one year old are bred in November. I have also been known to do another breeding in April for the very late doelings of the previous year.

Inbreeding and Keeping Records

You should learn to read the pedigrees for the breeds of goats that you have. You need to know for yourself that the new buck you are buying, to breed to your doelings, is not their uncle or cousin. Here is a very good definition of inbreeding and line-breeding: "Inbreeding is the mating together of closely related animals (such as brother to sister, son to dam, sire to daughter). It is done primarily to intensify the degree of homozygosity, or the similarity of the genes in the reproductive cells of the animals. Line-breeding is similar to inbreeding but involves the breeding of animals less closely related (such as cousins, and grandsire with granddaughters). It is done to conserve and perpetuate the good traits of certain outstanding breeding animals."[16]   However, although line-breeding may reinforce strong positive traits, it will also reinforce genetic flaws. Before you experiment with line-breeding, you need to do some solid research on the subject, *and* on the genetic heritage of your goats.

If you have more than one buck to choose from, it is important to know which buck you are going to breed to which does this year. You may even want to separate the does into different pens or pastures according to the buck they are to be bred to, and the month they are to be bred. This requires a little more planning, but it is easier than trying to decide who is related to whom when the buck has jumped the fence and you are trying to be sure he doesn't breed his daughters.

I keep careful records every year. In this age of computerization, most of us have access to a computer with a spread sheet program like Quatro or Excel. I would strongly advise keeping records of your breeding and your kidding. These records may seem like extra work now, but they will be invaluable to you in the future. When you are trying to decide whether or not to sell a buck, it would be nice to have records of the number of bucks vs. does he throws. If a particular genetic flaw is showing up repeatedly, it might be nice to have records so you can trace it back to a buck or a line of does. Do you remember how long the gestation usually runs for each of your does (a specific doe will run about the same each year), or how many saleable kids this doe has thrown in her lifetime? Do I always have to discount the kids out of this doe for some reason? Then why is she still here?

Here are some samples of my spread sheets for breeding and kidding:

#	Name	Buck	1st Bred	2nd Bred	Confirm	Date Due	Vaccinated?	Notes
46	ABBIE	MAX	27-Aug-97	18-Sep-97	MARKED	24-Jan-98	2-Jan-98	IN TO MAX 8-27-97; then 9-1-97 to 9-30
110	TOODLE	ZAZ	05-Sep-97	15-Sep-97	MARKED	02-Feb-98	2-Jan-98	IN TO ZAZ 8-27, then 9-1-97 to 9-30
130	MARTHA	MAX	06-Sep-97		D SAW	03-Feb-98	2-Jan-98	To Max 9-1-97 to 9-30
134	SASSY	NUG	06-Sep-97		MARKED	03-Feb-98	2-Jan-98	Hand Bred to Fab on 9-6-97 only
205	BELLA	ZAZ	06-Sep-97		G SAW	03-Feb-98	2-Jan-98	Hand Bred to ZAZ on 9-6-97 only

BUCK	Doe #	Name	Date Kidded	Kids in Ultrasound	DAYS PREG	KIDS BORN	AV WT	# OF M/F
MAX	46	ABBIE	18-Feb-98	3	153	3	10	1M 2F
ZAZ	110	TOODLE	12-Feb-98	2	149	2	8	1M 1F
MAX	130	MARTHA	4-Feb-98	3	151	2	7.3	1M 1F
NUG	134	SASSY	8-Feb-98	2	155	3	7.5	2M 1F
ZAZ	205	BELLA	7-Feb-98	2	154	2	10	1M 1F

It is impossible to include everything that is normally in these spreadsheets here, but they usually include columns on vaccinations and testing, and extensive notes about the actual kidding and the kids. I tend to write down if a kid has had any problems with fluid in its lungs, the kid's coloration, what kind of mother the doe was, if she had any trouble kidding or took an unusual length of time, etc. I also use a data management program to keep track of pedigrees, vet visits, show results, birth dates, etc.

'Non-Breeders'

Goats are incredibly prolific animals. A truly sterile goat is relatively unusual. However, it can happen. If you have a buck that won't breed, or who can't get the does pregnant when he breeds, it could be one of several difficulties besides sterility. Many bucks will not breed out of season, and if they do breed, their sperm count is not high enough for the does to conceive. The buck who doesn't breed may also be too young, have been overused recently, may be in some kind of pain (back pain, or hip pain is pretty common), be over-stressed by being moved, etc. However, the most common problem with a buck who doesn't breed, is poor nutrition. A breeding buck must have a good ration that includes enough energy, protein, vitamins and minerals to keep him breeding. If all of the above issues have been seen to, your only option is to call a veterinarian to see if there is some abnormality.

If a doe will not breed, or if she breeds and breeds but does not get pregnant, she may have cystic ovaries. This is a fairly common condition which is now treatable by a simple injection from the veterinarian. Other reasons for not breeding are; the wrong season of the year, already pregnant, her heats may just be very hard to see, malnutrition, recent kidding, a heavy current milk yield, a false pregnancy, having been treated with hormonal drugs, or she may have an infection. Also, does can be born 'intersexed' or a 'hermaphrodite'. This condition, unfortunately, does occur. Sometimes, you can see a hermaphrodite if you look in the lower end of her vulva. There will be a small abnormal growth just inside the lower section of the vulva. Also, her teats will be small and hard, instead of large and pliable. If your doe is not breeding, but you can't see the external abnormalities described above, you should have her examined by your veterinarian.

Genetic Flaws to be Aware of

Genetic traits are passed from one generation to the next through genes. The study of genetics is fascinating, and much too complex to do it justice here. However, there are several very good books on the subject, some of them are bound to be available at your local library. I would suggest that you take some time and look it up. If a trait is only in one parent, it will probably show up in half the offspring. If it is recessive in one parent, it will still show up, as a recessive gene, in ¼ of the offspring. If you breed together two goats with a recessive gene, it becomes dominant in ¼ of the offspring. Goat people often say that recessive traits carried in the father will not show up until those kids have kids. In other words, much is blamed on the grandfather. If you look at the way genetics work, that might not be too far off.

It is also said that it takes three generations to breed out a trait. That would only be true if the trait is not carried as a recessive gene in each generation, in one or the other parent. In other words, it can be difficult to completely remove an undesirable trait from your herd, once you have it.

The next subject then becomes, what do you define as an undesirable trait? The judges whom I have consulted come from both Dairy and Boer goat judging backgrounds. The traits discussed below are things that will count against you in a show ring. It is very important not to get the show ring confused with the pasture! If you are raising meat animals, and you can purchase good meat stock for less money because it has some trait that the breeder sees as undesirable, but that you don't see as a problem for your meat herd, it would be foolish not to purchase that animal! As a matter of fact, if you are putting together a meat herd and can do a larger portion of it with 'flawed' fullblood meat goats, you are going to have one great meat production herd! Just be sure the 'flaws' don't get in the way of production, and you don't sell your goats that carry these undesirable traits to people who are looking for breeding stock.

Now, do <u>not</u> go out and drown all your goats because you read in this book that something is a 'flaw'! That is not why I am including this section. I am including it so that you, my reader, are educated. I want you to be able to make educated, informed choices, and buy that 'flawed' goat on purpose, not through ignorance. If you need to cull a 'flawed' animal, either educate your buyer about what he is buying, and why he might or might not want to buy it, or just butcher the animal. I would like to hear someday, that some producers of breeding stock stopped producing goats carrying 'undesirable traits' because they found out about them in this book.

<u>Consider what you need and what will work toward *your* goals for *your* herd</u>.

Color: Color is listed as an issue in most breed standards. It is also mainly a matter of taste. If you are breeding for expensive breeding stock, you must know what colors are acceptable to your breed, and breed for those colors exclusively. If you are raising meat, color makes no difference at all unless the meat market you are catering to requires some attribute that includes hair color.

Jaw: Problems with the jaw are important problems. Goats can be born with a face that doesn't fit well together, or is twisted. They can also have a poor bite that does not allow them to chew properly. Goats do not have teeth on the upper jaw. They have a hard plate of gums. The teeth on the lower jaw are intended to cut against that hard plate like a pair of scissors. When you open the lips on a goat and look into her mouth, the teeth should meet the gums right on the edge, or they should scissor directly in front of the gums. The judges that I have consulted say that they allow a maximum of about 3/8 inch of space between the gums and teeth in an adult goat. The bite will change as a goat gets older. Generally, the lower jaw grows farther out in front of the gums (overshot). So young animals need to have good bites if they are going to compete when they are older.

Ears: The way an ear hangs, or the color of an ear, are factors of breed preference. Again, this may greatly affect your breeding stock, but it should not affect your meat herd. However, there is a genetic deformity where the ear is folded top to bottom all the way into the ear canal, in effect, nearly closing the ear. There is also a tendency in long eared goats to be born with 'uterine molding' that gives the ear a similar appearance to an ear with the actual deformity, but which is not actually a defect. If you can open the ear at birth and flatten it out along the side of the kid's head, it is uterine molding. Consequences to a meat herd with deformed ears? Moisture and bugs might get trapped in the ear causing infections.

Flaws of the front end assembly: There are several 'flaws' concerning the way the shoulders and chest are put together. If the shoulder blades are not snug into the body, the goat walks with a sort of unhinged gait. If the condition is too pronounced, the goat may have trouble getting back and forth to the pasture. The chest and heartgirth can be too narrow, or actually appear 'caved in'. Meat goats should have deep, broad chests to have the lung capacity to walk back and forth to pasture, and to carry more width through to the loin and the hind quarters.

Loin: The loin is the most important cut of meat. Therefore, it is important that the loin be long and wide. Now, if you are not raising show stock, can you have some goats with short, wide loins and some with longer loins? Of course! Does that doe with the short loin go out every year and bring in two big kids for the market? Does your buck have a longer loin to compensate?

Legs: Goats walk on their legs so, in my opinion, legs need to be right. Some goats have knock knees in the front. Other goats have rear legs that are 'posty' in the hock. A 'posty' leg is one that is not bent at all in the hock when the goat is standing naturally. When a goat gets older, or is in the last month of her pregnancy, a 'posty' leg may actually try to bend the wrong way at the hock.

Either knock knees or posty hocks may make it difficult
for your goats to walk long distances.

Teats: Boer goats generally have four teats. They were
originally bred to raise high multiple kids, and have
enough teats to take care of them. There is nothing wrong
with four teats, in a Boer! (Six or eight teats are not good.)
However, there is a 'flaw' where two teats are so close
together that they actually come out of the body on one
base, and split at the end of the teat. This is called split
teats, or fish teats (because the teat resembles a fish tail).
This condition is not acceptable in the show ring, and may
have some repercussions in the pasture as well. The
theory suggests that either kids might not be able to get
their mouth around the teat at all, or they may suck on
one half of the teat while the other half drips milk into
their nose.

Split Scrotum: Some bucks have a solid bag or scrotum
around their testicles, and others have a split in the bag
between the testicles. Some breeders say that a split
scrotum allows the testicles to stay cooler, increasing
fertility. Other breeders say that ticks and insects will
lodge in the split causing the buck a very painful death.
At this point, the show ring in the United States is
allowing a 1 inch split in the scrotum of an adult buck.
Are you raising show stock? Do you live in an area that
has a lot of ticks?

Low Fertility and Non-Breeders: Poor   breeders   or
sterile goats are very rare. For some reason, some of the
first Boers to come into this country carried this very
serious 'flaw'. I don't hear much about them any more,
but I'm sure you will agree with me when I suggest that if
you have meat goats that consistently produce non-
breeders, you need find out who is carrying the gene and
make some nice Chevon steaks with the offender.

Alternative Breeding Methods

In this age of computers and high tech medicine, even goat breeding has become a technical field all in itself. Some veterinarians specialize in 'Alternative Breeding Methods' for goats. One such method is Embryo Transfer. In Embryo Transfer the veterinarian 'super-ovulates' the doe that you want to produce extra kids. Then he artificially cycles some 'recipient' does to come into heat at the same time as the 'donor' doe. The owner breeds the donor doe, and six days later, the veterinarian moves her fertilized eggs to the recipient does, who then carry the donor's kids to term for her. This process is relatively expensive, and must be done by an experienced specialist. In many areas, the veterinarian is just not available.

Picture 22: And 150 days later you have bunches of dairy goats kidding with little fullblood Boer kids?[*]

---

[*] This picture donated by Kids-R-Us Goat Farm from Uvalde, Texas

I write a little magazine column with the help of a friend of mine, Annette Maze. The focus of the column is the differences in goat raising between the northern and southern United States. I have included a few of these articles in this book, because they are fun and informative. This one goes into a little more depth about embryo transfer and artificial insemination:

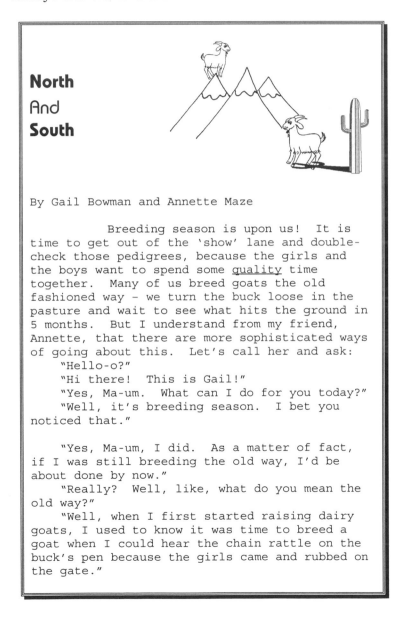

North
And
South

By Gail Bowman and Annette Maze

        Breeding season is upon us! It is time to get out of the 'show' lane and double-check those pedigrees, because the girls and the boys want to spend some quality time together. Many of us breed goats the old fashioned way – we turn the buck loose in the pasture and wait to see what hits the ground in 5 months. But I understand from my friend, Annette, that there are more sophisticated ways of going about this. Let's call her and ask:
    "Hello-o?"
    "Hi there! This is Gail!"
    "Yes, Ma-um. What can I do for you today?"
    "Well, it's breeding season. I bet you noticed that."

    "Yes, Ma-um, I did. As a matter of fact, if I was still breeding the old way, I'd be about done by now."
    "Really? Well, like, what do you mean the old way?"
    "Well, when I first started raising dairy goats, I used to know it was time to breed a goat when I could hear the chain rattle on the buck's pen because the girls came and rubbed on the gate."

"Oh. I guess you don't breed that way any
more, huh?"

"No Ma-um. Things are a little more
refined than that these days. Of course there
are still some girls that get bred 'in person',
so to speak, but most of mine are either embryo
transfer or artificial insemination these
days."

"Really? Well, I just don't seem to be
able to learn to do AI. Do you have any
advice?"

"Yes, Ma-um. You wait until the doe comes
into heat, and the buck will mount her. But
don't let him breed her, honey. You can use a
big trash sack with holes cut in for his legs,
and then put some duct tape around his chest,
for a buck condom, you know. Or you can have
one of your bucks surgically sterilized. Then,
after he starts mounting her, count four hours.
Then check your doe. When her vaginal
excretion is the consistency of stringy cheese,
and the cervix is open, it is time to breed
her."

"Oh. Well, I heard that you should use a
buck for follow up in 21 days so you don't take
a chance on missing a season."

"Yes, Ma-um. That is just common sense.
But let me tell you, I once knew a gal that had
100% success with her AI program."

"Really? Like, how did she do that?"

"Well, honey, she just used her old
'sterile' buck to kinda 'tamp in' that semen."

"Oh. Well, that seems like a good idea,
and you say it worked?"

"Yes, Ma-um. She had a 100% pregnancy
rate. It never seemed to bother her much that
she was AI-ing with Boer semen and all her kids
looked like black Nubians."

"Now, wait a minute. Why would they be
black?"

"Well, honey, I'm not at liberty to say,
exactly, but that *was* the color of her old
sterile buck."

"Oh, well, maybe I don't want to use that
particular method. You know, the other day I
was in a restaurant talking about goats. And
suddenly I looked around and the entire
restaurant was staring at me. I don't know
what their problem was!"

"Really? Well, can you remember what you were you talking about at the time?"

"Like, just breeding stuff. I think I was just telling my friend about that little trick you told me to increase the odds of the doe settling after AI."

"Oh, which tip was that?"

"You know, like, the one where you massage their clitoris for 30 seconds after you AI."

"Yes, Ma-um. That'll do it!"

"Do what?"

"Just think about it for a while, honey, you'll get it."

"Oh! You mean it was the… Oh! Well, now I'm embarrassed! You know I never used to say words like that before I raised goats? I *was* a good Id-e-ho girl. Now look what's happened to me!"

"Yes, Ma-um! Anyway, I don't AI as much as I used to, because I do mostly embryo transfer now."

"Wow! And, like, what's involved in that?"

"Well, Ma-um, you have to find yourself a really good veterinarian, first. Then he will give you a schedule to follow, and you have to be absolutely faithful to that schedule. First you have to put in a vaginal implant and leave it in for a certain number of days. Then you give your donor does a series of shots. Then you have to pull out the implants and watch for heat in all your does. Then you carefully write down when everyone went into heat and who you bred your donors to. This is the most reliable way to increase your herd with quality animals. It is very exciting!"

"I should say so! Then what happens?"

"Well, honey, then the doctor shows up, and you have to shave and wash the tummies on your does. Then he opens them up and counts how many little blisters there are on their ovaries. If there are no blisters, there are no eggs. Did you know that?"

"No! How would I know a thing like that? Then what?"

"Well, honey, if everything is just the way they like, then they put a little needle into one side of the donor's oviduct and flush some saline water through the needle and back out another little hole on the other end of her uterus. Then they look at the water under a microscope and see how many eggs are fertilized and how many are no good. Then they sew up the donor and bring in the recipient. They do the same thing to her. They open her up and count blisters on her ovaries, then put a needle into the top of her uterus and sloosh in two little fertilized eggs in some of the water."

"Then what"

"That's it. They sew up the recipient and away she goes. In a few minutes she wakes up and goes back out to the pasture just like nothing ever happened."

"Wow! Really? She doesn't like need to take a week off work and take Valium or anything? Huh. Well, is there something that you do to get a better success rate?"

"Yes, Ma-um. I never leave them alone to wake up because they could choke, and I always give them a probiotic after they are awake to help them to get their rumens started again."

"And that's it? And 150 days later you have bunches of dairy goats kidding with little fullblood Boer kids? Wow! You know, it's pretty hard to find a veterinarian up here that will do the work. But you do this every year, don't you?"

"Yes, Ma-um. There are advantages to living in the South. Gotta go! I'll talk to y'all later. Bye!"

Artificial Insemination

Artificial Insemination is not even close to the leading edge of technology any more, but for most of us, it is as close as we are going to come. There are many excellent reasons to learn to AI. For one thing, an AI tank doesn't tear down your fences and smell up your living room! Even if you are breeding by AI, though, you have to have a reliable way to tell when your does are in heat. For many people, that still means at least borrowing a buck for the girls to flirt with.

To learn AI you will need the following equipment:
- ✓ A semen tank.
- ✓ Semen.
- ✓ A microscope is very handy to check the viability of the semen on the spot.
- ✓ At least two large and two small speculums. A speculum looks like a test tube with a hole in both ends. It works kind of like a funnel to get your AI gun into the doe's vagina.
- ✓ An AI light so you can see what you are doing.
- ✓ Straw tweezers to hold the straw of semen.
- ✓ A thermos or a thaw can to thaw the straw of semen in.
- ✓ A thermometer for the water in your thaw can.
- ✓ A straw cutter to get the end off the straw.
- ✓ An insemination gun or French goat gun.
- ✓ Disposable sheaths to go over your insemination gun and needles if you have a needle gun.
- ✓ Non-spermicidal AI lubricant.
- ✓ Paper Towels.
- ✓ Warm soapy water.
- ✓ A heating pad for cold weather. No, not for you, for the semen!

One of the most important things to understand about artificial insemination is the timing. A doe is in heat for 12 to 36 hours. The egg is not actually released until 6 hours after a doe comes into standing heat. The best time to AI is 12 to 18 hours after the doe comes into standing heat. You have to remember that the idea is to get a live sperm into contact with a viable egg. Both the egg and the sperm are short lived and fragile. If you have tried to AI with no success, you may start to wonder how the bucks seem to manage it without even trying! But they deliver very large amounts of fresh sperm into a perfect environment. You are working with a small amount of sperm that is not fresh and needs to make a temperature shift before it can be delivered.

Artificial Insemination is a skill that I cannot possibly teach you here. I strongly recommend that you have a real live person teach this to you. There are also videos and books available on the subject. One of the best booklets that I have found is put out by Magnum Semen Works.

Very basically, this is how it is done: Fill your thaw container with 95 degree F water to just below the height of a straw. Restrain the doe, then wash her vulva and the area around it with warm sudsy water. Wash with a downward motion being careful not to contaminate your paper towel by bringing it in contact with the area around the anus. Dry her off with a clean paper towel. Then wash and dry your hands.

Open the semen tank and bring the canister, with the semen you want to use, just close enough to the rim of the tank to be able to reach the straw you want with your tweezers. Quickly put the straw into the thaw jar with the plugged end up. It is now safe for 15 minutes.

Now warm up your gun by rubbing it in your clean hand or putting it inside your clothing. Now pull the trigger of the gun out 6" and insert your straw cotton plug end first. Hold your straw out a little and cut off the other end with your straw cutter.

Now insert the gun and straw into the sheath with just enough pressure to seat the straw. Put the rubber donut on the gun to lock it in place, wrap it in a clean paper towel and place it in a warm heating pad.

Now lubricate the speculum with non-spermicidal gel, and insert it in her vulva with the off-centered end going in first, and pointed up. You will encounter an obstruction called the hiloc, so just work it gently upward and downward to get past. Now aim upward to avoid hitting the urethra which is at the bottom of the vaginal canal.

If your doe is in heat, she should not be terribly offended by the goings – on. Place your AI light inside the speculum and look for the cervix. You are looking for a small puckered 'nose' at the back of the vagina, at about 5 to 7 o'clock, with a black or dark red hole in the center of it. Once you find the cervix, catch it in the hole in the end of the speculum and 'lock' it in with a gentle pressure.

The mucus you should be having to fight should be very thick, and the cervix should be bright red with a black dot in the middle.

Now take your gun out and expel any air that is in the end of the straw. Insert the gun into the speculum and into the opening of the cervix. Now place another sheath with 1 ½ inches marked off on the end of it next to your gun and against the cervix. You should only go into the cervix past four rings (the cervix has rings that you must go through to penetrate it) or 1 ½ inches. Don't go any further because you could injure the doe if you go too far.
Now draw back a little so that you aren't trying to put semen into tissue, and depress the plunger of the gun slowly, half way. Now slowly deposit the rest of the semen as you pull the gun back out of the cervix.

Gently remove the speculum and the gun. Insert your thumb slightly into the vagina and gently massage the clitoris for 5 seconds. The clitoris is located just inside the vulva and on the bottom of the vaginal floor.[17]

It is a good idea to watch your doe to see if she comes back into heat, or if you are afraid you won't catch her in heat again, just put her in with a buck in about two weeks. Of course, putting her in with the buck does not give you the chance to try AI again this year, but you will know she is pregnant. You could also wait 40 days, and if she has not come back into heat, have her ultrasounded so you know for sure if she is pregnant and you can make an informed decision.

Kidding

I think everyone's favorite part of raising goats is kidding time. You may not enjoy the waiting, or the stress of making sure all the kids are OK, but we all look forward to kidding season anyway. Kidding season means production (it also means cute little kids). Productions means profit, and profit is a good thing.

I just like baby goats. I love to make spread sheets to keep track of the new arrivals, and then watch those spread sheets fill up! I love to watch the kids take that first *jump*! I love to watch the kids as they go out to the pasture for the first time, and I love to sell big healthy kids to happy customers.

But before we can do any of those things, we need to safely kid out our goats.

When and Where to Kid Your Goats

Your goats will need a place to have their kids. This can be a section of the main barn that is separated by some temporary fencing, or a special kidding stall, but it should be a place where the mothers-to-be can get away by themselves. If a goat kids out in the pasture or in a community pen, she will still look for a place to be alone, and if she can't find it, she may panic.

I always try to have a good idea of the due date, so that I can bring my does in about 4 days before they are due.

Picture 23: I love to watch the kids take that first *jump*!*

We have some small pens that we kid out in. Some are in a small barn, and some are outside. If the doe is lucky enough to have a stall in the barn, she will be in a pen that is about 6 foot by 8 foot, has plywood sides, and holes in the gate so that she can put her head outside the pen to get water and grain. I don't like to leave the water bucket in the pen because the doe might inadvertently have her kid right in the bucket! That would be terrible. If the doe is outside, she is using a pen that is built around an old calf house. These pens are about 12 foot long and about 6

---

* This picture donated by Sand Creek Boer Goats from Shelly, Idaho.

foot wide. Each pen has a divided section of calf house so the Mother can get inside. The indoor part is about 4 foot wide and 8 foot long. The calf house is only about 4 foot high at the highest point, but the goats don't seem to mind. This arrangement does make it harder for me to get in and help, though.

I try to use some kind of listening or video monitoring system so that I know when a doe is kidding. They usually make some noise, so a baby monitor works pretty well, if your barn is close enough to the house for the signal to reach.

No, everyone isn't this careful, but I like to see my profits hit the ground and know that they are alright. It doesn't make sense to me to lose kids and/or mothers because no one was there to help with the sack, or straighten out a leg. And I *like* to be there. It is fun to watch. You have waited for 5 months to see what is in the package, I think it is only right to be there when the package is unwrapped!

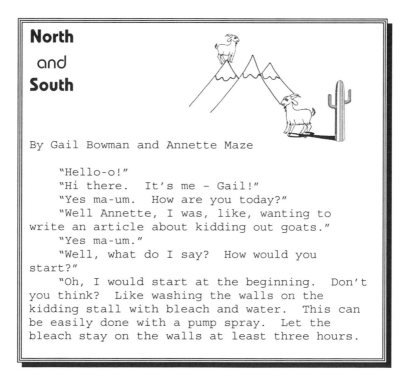

North
and
South

By Gail Bowman and Annette Maze

"Hello-o!"
"Hi there. It's me – Gail!"
"Yes ma-um. How are you today?"
"Well Annette, I was, like, wanting to write an article about kidding out goats."
"Yes ma-um."
"Well, what do I say? How would you start?"
"Oh, I would start at the beginning. Don't you think? Like washing the walls on the kidding stall with bleach and water. This can be easily done with a pump spray. Let the bleach stay on the walls at least three hours.

Then mix Tide and water in the sprayer and
wash the walls once more. This is virtually
work free. Be sure the floor is clean and
sprinkled with ag lime. Cover this with clean
hay or straw and you're ready to go."

"Yes, that's good, but I think I would have
to start with a clean stall that has had a
chance to stand empty and get good and frozen,
then swept out and Cloroxed. You know, in the
winter here, the cold would probably kill a lot
of stuff. Then, I would probably use a weed
burner to be sure it's 'torched out' good
before we straw it."

"Yes ma-um, but not everyone lives in the
'frozen wastes of the north', or kids out in
zero degree weather. My system will work
anywhere. And how often are you going to tell
people to check their does once they bring them
into the barn?"

"Oh, I almost never have to check my mama
goats."

"Why's that? I know you don't leave them
out to kid in the snow!"

"No, I bring them into the barn, like,
about four days before they're due. Then I
just watch them on the security camera on the
'goat channel' on my TV. I never miss a
kidding."

"Well honey, the rest of the world still
sets our alarm and walks out to the barn to
check those does every two hours! However, my
husband did buy me an intercom system. I've
found that a trained ear can usually hear a
goat kidding."

"Wow! How strange! But we both can agree
to, like, save up feed sacks to kid out on, and
newspapers to dry off those cute little kids,
right?"

"Yes ma-um"

"Then, when the temperature is under about
ten or twenty degrees, you do carry around a
blow dryer to help dry them off, don't you?"

"Well, when the temperature in Texas gets
under ten degrees, I'll be sure to run right
out and buy me a blow dryer! Now, don't forget
to tell folks to use 7% iodine to dip umbilical
cords and feet, not 1%. And to keep dental
floss or umbilical clamps in their pockets in
case they get one that keeps bleeding."

"Do you know what happens to 7% iodine when it is below freezing outside and it comes in contact with a warm kid? It vaporizes! I use it, but I keep it out from under my face! Boy howdy! That'll make your eyes water! Then, I think, I need to be sure everyone, like, cleans off the mother's teats with warm water, or a wet wipe, or newspaper, then milks out a few squirts of milk to get the bacteria out of the end of the teat."

"Yes ma-um, that's pretty basic. Don't forget to let the dam get lots of licking in first, or she won't take that kid. Also, don't feed it any other goat's milk, or she won't want it either, you know. And if the kid won't nurse, you need to stomach tube it or bottle feed it some of the dam's milk with a Pritchert nipple!"

"You know, I've found that it is worth while to buy a bottle of 50% Dextrose for IV use. Then, if the kid is weak, you can just put about 1cc in their cheek with a syringe (take the needle off first), and they tend to perk right up."

"Yes ma-um. But nobody is going to have a chance to feed that kid if the dam dropped it in a 5-gallon water bucket. Be sure everyone knows to hang up their water buckets or put them on the other side of the fence. And, another thing, if the dam paws at her baby she could hurt or kill it! If the dam is pawing her kids, you can put the kids in a box outside the fence for a little while, or give them a half a dog kennel, up side down, so they can be safe until they are strong enough to get out of the way."

"You know, I've found that just, like, putting a ten or twelve inch board across one end of the pen, creating a 'play pen' helps to let Mom get away from the kids for a little while, and keeps the kids under the heat. I seem to have calmer mothers when they know they can step away."

"Yes ma-um. And don't forget to remind folks to watch for the afterbirth. Many people find out the hard way that retained afterbirth takes its toll. People should do their very best to save those little Boer kids. Do not

just trust the dam. Hold the kids up to the
teat and be sure they nurse. Learn how the
stomach should feel and how it should look when
it is truly full. Listen for that awful "I'm
hungry" cry. Tell people to remember that just
because an udder is big, does not mean it
actually is making milk. Edema has killed many
kids. The time kids take in the first few days
will pay for itself a thousand times over!"
     "Don't you, like, give the moms anything
after they kid? I always give mine a little
Karo Syrup in warm water. As a matter of fact,
on those really cold nights, quite a bit of
almost hot water seems to be appreciated."
     "Yes ma-um, but Gatoraide works well too.
And I always worm mine the day they kid, at the
same time I give the kids their shots, so I
don't forget."
     "Wow! What a lot of work! I bet people
raising goats for meat won't want to do it."
     "Yes Honey, but they would be well to spend
a little time in the barn and reap the rewards
in extra income, and the folks raising quality
breeding stock will want to know the correct
procedure. Every kid lost is five months of
feeding the dam and another year till she
produces again! One more thing! Don't forget
to warn people about Floppy Kid Syndrome!
That's one killer we should all know as much
about as we can."
     "OK, but maybe I'll have to do some
research and just write an article on FKS some
day."
     "That's a great idea, but be sure to call
and talk it over with me first! Bye now!" ♥

When will my Goats Kid?

A lot has been said about predicting when goats will kid. I
have read that goats will wait for good weather to kid. If
there were a study on this subject, my ranch would be the
one used to prove that goats wait for <u>bad</u> weather to kid.
We have a saying around here, "If there are goats in the
<u>barn, and the snow starts to fly</u>, you'd better start running

♥ This 'North and South' appeared in <u>The Goat Rancher Magazine</u> in
April 1997

for the barn." This leads me to suggest that goats are more likely to kid if there is a <u>change</u> in the weather. It has been suggested that it is the change in the barometric pressure that causes a goat to go into labor. Or, maybe, it was just the right time.

Another interesting saying I have heard is, "Goats don't kid at night." Well, I have a friend that tells me that her does always kid at 2:00 in the morning! I didn't believe her until I bought some goats from her that were near their kidding date. They both kidded at 2:00 in the morning! This really got me curious. So I kept track of kidding times on my ranch. Here are the results of a two year study on my ranch:

Goats that kidded between 6am and 10am:	17
Goats that kidded between 12 noon and 2pm:	40
Goats that kidded between 4pm and 5pm:	13
Goats that kidded between 7pm and 8pm:	<u>12</u>
Total goats kidded:	82

No goats kidded outside these times except one doe who had such terrible problems that she almost didn't make it; she kidded at 1 o'clock in the morning. Conclusions? Perhaps altitude *and* barometric pressure influence kidding times. On my ranch, we tend to pay more attention around 12 noon.

Labor and Kidding

The normal gestation time for goats is 145 to 155 days. Most goats will kid between 149 and 151 days. The last month or two before your doe is due, you should raise the sugar content of her feed a little to avoid pregnancy toxemia and to help her kids to grow to their full potential (see 'Pregnancy Toxemia' in the chapter of this book called "Health Needs and Potential Problems"). You can do this by adding a little molassified grain to her feed ration, especially if you have been feeding plain alfalfa without grain.

For the purposes of this discussion, I am going to assume that you are kidding in a barn or shed. Many goats kid just fine out in the pasture, under a bush or behind a wall. And for the breeder who is raising 600 meat goats, you will probably see the doe stay to herself, or refuse to go out to pasture at all that day. Whether you are kidding in the pasture or in a kidding pen, the following will help you to know that all is progressing as it should.

There are many signs that your goat is coming into labor. However, just like in women, every goat and every labor is different. I have had three children and have never spoken to another women who has had an experience just like any of mine. I said that to say this: These are the signs that your doe is coming close to kidding. Not every goat will show every sign, and you have to be watching pretty closely to see any of them. So use them as mile markers, and don't worry if you never see her do some of them.

- ✓ Your doe will 'bag up'. Starting as much as weeks before the birth, her bag will begin to fill. If your doe is a dairy doe that has been bred for generations to produce huge amounts of milk, she may (in extreme cases) even need to be milked before the kids are born to avoid mastitis. The problem with this is that she won't have any colostrum for her kids, so early milking is to be avoided except in emergencies. The last few hours before she gives birth, the doe's bag will suddenly get *very* full and tight.
- ✓ Some people feel the doe's abdomen for the kids. If you are good at this, the kids can be felt on the right side of the doe (the left is the rumen). If you can still feel the kids, the doe will probably not kid for at least 12 hours.[18]
- ✓ The doe will 'loosen up' before she kids. This term refers to the condition of the vulva. A goat's vulva is normally kind of puckered as though it has a draw string in the middle. When they are in heat, or especially when they are getting ready to kid, the vulva will get loose and open.
- ✓ A few nights before the birth your goat may display what we call 'dead goat syndrome'. She will fall into such a deep sleep that you may wonder if she is still alive.

✓ Goats, and people, don't just wake up from a nap and find that they have had a baby. They get nervous, worry and 'nest'. With me it was always scrubbing the bathroom floor the day before the baby arrived. With goats it is usually finding a place to lie down that she has never laid in before, then pushing all the straw out of the way so she can lay on the nice clean dirt (which is never under the straw in kidding pens, but she doesn't seem to realize that). This is one reason it is often said that kidding in the pasture can be more sanitary.

✓ She will walk around and try to stand with her front feet on a little higher level than her back feet. She will not sleep, act uncomfortable and be generally unhappy.

✓ The perfect pear shape that she has been maintaining for weeks (with her belly as the fat bottom of the pear and her tail as the stem) will suddenly disappear. Her right side will shrink or even hollow out as the kids travel 'down' into the birth canal. She will probably kid within a few hours after this happens.

✓ There is a ligament that runs from the pin bones to the dorsal process. When a goat is getting ready to kid, this ligament will move out of the way to allow the kids to get between the pelvic bones. To feel for this ligament, you can put your hand on the doe's tail head. Measure about two to three inches up her rump toward her hip bones. Try to put your fingers around her spine at this point. If you can't, she is not ready. When you can feel your own fingers and thumb touching (except for skin and fur) around her spine, she will kid within twelve hours.

✓ Your doe's tail may seem to become 'unhinged' as it lays along her back and, usually, a little to one side.

✓ She will be nervous and get up, walk around, kick at her nest, lay down, bounce right back up, walk around, lay down on her other side, bounce back up, walk around... She is in early labor.

✓ The doe will look at her belly as though it belongs to someone else. She may kick at it or rub it with her head.

✓ One of the most obvious signs is that there will be a long string of clear yellowish mucus hanging almost to the floor. Some goats have a discharge for several

days before they give birth, but if you have been watching, you will see that this is different.
- ✓ Eventually she will lay down and give a big push. Then jump up and walk around. Then lay down and give another push. Many does become very vocal about this time. Eventually she will get serious.
- ✓ She may remain standing, or more likely, she may lay down, but she will start to give serious pushes – one after another. When your doe reaches this stage, start timing her. She should not be allowed to push like this for more than 30 minutes without making progress. Progress means that you should be able to see something coming out. If she gets past 30 minutes, and nothing is happening, you should be considering that she might have a problem.

If all goes well (which, by the way, it usually does with healthy goats) you will soon see a bag of water protruding from the vulva. Just leave her alone and let her work it out. Soon the water will break or be expelled and another bag will appear. This one has a kid in it. If you are watching you will soon see two little hooves and a nose. Often the tongue is hanging out. That is normal. It usually takes a while for the doe to stretch enough to free the kid's forehead, especially in first time kidders. I like to let her work her way through this stage on her own. You can help the kid out if you clean the mucous off its nose at this point. However, if she is tiring, or has been working on it for more than about 45 minutes (from the time you see the first bag of water to the time the forehead is free), it will help her if you straighten the kid's legs out in front of it. This is a little bit dangerous if she thrashes around at all, because the kid's legs could be broken by getting bashed against a wall. However, the kid usually just slides out at this point, and it is all over in a matter of minutes.

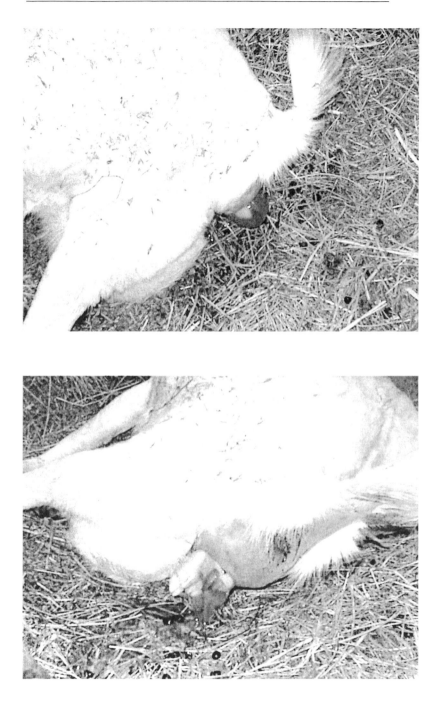

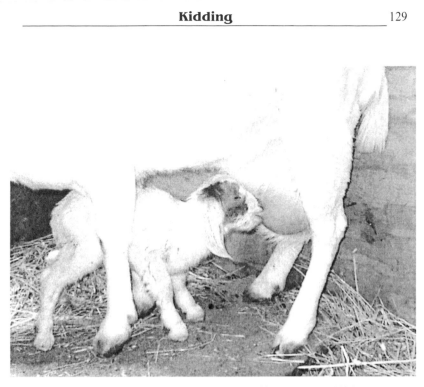

Picture 24: Plate 1: ... **another bag will appear. This one has a kid in it. Plate 2: If you are watching you will soon see two little hooves and a nose. Often the tongue is hanging out. Plate 3: Once the shoulders are born the kid will usually just slide out in one slurp. Plate 4: Then, pull the newspaper with the kid on it around to the mother's head and let her lick the kid. Plate 5: It is very important that kids get a good drink of colostrum as soon as possible after birth.** *

---

* My thanks to Serendipity for allowing me to photograph her delivery! These pictures from Bowman Boer Ranch in Twin Falls, Idaho.

ᵁSometimes, a little help is required if the doe just can't get things to progress. You can pull downward on the kid's front legs, but be sure to do it only when she is pushing. Working with the mother will help to keep her from being injured by your assistance. Remember that this is a baby animal, and you can hurt it, and the mother, if you get over-zealous.

Once the shoulders are born, the kid will usually just slide out in one slurp. I like to have some clean newspaper for it to land on. (By the way, I don't use the colored sections of the newspaper, because I have heard that they contain harmful chemicals.) The very first thing you must do is to clear the kid's mouth and nose of mucous. You can use a clean cloth or towel, or a human baby bulb syringe. The umbilical cord will usually just break. If you feel you need to cut it for some reason, you will want to have some dental floss, clean twine or umbilical clamps to put on the kid side of the cut, because a cut cord will bleed. Sometimes a cord will bleed anyway, so it is good to have something in your kidding kit to put on it, just in case you need it.

Then, pull the newspaper with the kid on it around to the mother's head and let her lick the kid. After she has had some time to lick the kid all over, pick it up, and dip the cord and the little ends of the hooves in the 7% iodine that you have poured into a small container for this purpose. I keep baby food jars around to put the iodine in. Just put the cord in the jar, and tip the kid back so that the iodine covers all the way to the little belly. This is not a fun thing to have to do as it may burn your eyes, but it will cauterize the entrance areas so that bacteria can't get into the kid's system. I am so sensitive to the iodine, that I get some extra paper ready first, then dip over the old paper, put the kid on the fresh paper, pull it over to the mom, and remove the old paper to a trash bin immediately so that the iodine isn't in the pen where I am.

ᵁ PLEASE NOTE: I am not a veterinarian and have no veterinary training. It is not my intention to give medical advice. Before you follow any suggestion printed in this book that might be construed as medical advice, ALWAYS seek the advice of a qualified veterinarian.

If the weather is very cold, and the mom has had several minutes to bond with her kid, I will dry the kid off with clean newspaper. Sometimes I even wrap the dried off kid in a clean towel and then give him back to the mom, making sure that she can still lick his head and tail. (I don't use towels to begin with, because that mucous can be really hard to get out of your laundry.)

Now it is time for mom to get busy and have the next kid. What if the first kid wants to get up and nurse? If the first kid will just lay there obediently and let mom get on with it – great! But sometimes it has been 20 minutes and I can't get the doe to focus on the job at hand, so I have a little trick. If you wrap the kid in a nice dry towel and put him, tail first, into an empty five gallon bucket, mom can still lick him and he will usually fall asleep! Now brother can be born. This usually takes just a few minutes. Mom gets to lick brother so she knows he is hers too, then kid number one can come out and have a drink. It is very important that kids get a good drink of colostrum as soon as possible after birth, and certainly within an hour of birth. *Colostrum is very important* because it contains antibodies and vitamins that the kids <u>must</u> have! There is a period of about 10 minutes right after birth during which most kids just can't coordinate sucking on a teat. So if it hasn't been very long since the kid was born, and you are cold and want to go in but you can't get the kid to suck, zip up your coat, let mom lick him for another five minutes, and try again.

What happens if you had expected 3 kids and the doe only has one or two? Sometimes goats can have a dead kid, or one who has trouble being born. Pay attention to your doe. Does she look like she is done? Is she still straining? Have you seen the afterbirth? If you really think she may not be done, it is better to check, than to lose the doe. A doe with a dead kid in her will become toxic and die very quickly. To check, an experienced goat raiser told me this trick: "To determine if another kid is still inside, face the same direction as the doe. Clasp your hands together around the doe just in front of the udder. Pull up gently, and drop your hands. If another kid is present, you will feel it through the abdominal wall at the drop."[19] If this doesn't work for you, or you are still unsure, you can follow the directions in this chapter under "Delivery Problems, What if the goat has been pushing for more than 30 minutes and nothing is coming out?"

Taking Care of the New Mother

After kidding, the new mother could use some sugar in her system.   A couple tablespoons of Karo syrup or molasses in a little warm water, or some Gatoraide, or some of the pre-made Goat Drench that is available now, would be a help to her. Be sure that she has plenty of fresh water to drink, and that it is warm if the weather is cold, and give her some good quality hay. She probably won't be interested in eating for a while, but will need the nutrition when she finds the time.

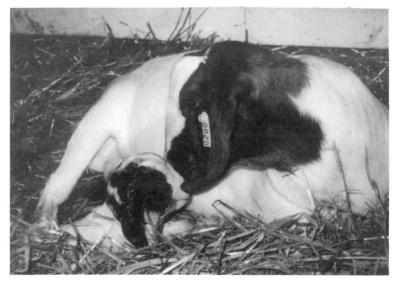

Picture 25: Keep the kids and new mothers by themselves for three days.[*]

Be sure to watch for the afterbirth. A doe should drop her afterbirth within a couple of hours after kidding. Just

[*] This picture donated by Wynneshire Farm in Ridgefield, Washington.

pick up the afterbirth with some newspaper, and throw it away. If it has been more than 12 hours and you are sure the afterbirth hasn't dropped (you have to watch, because the does will eat the afterbirth), call your veterinarian. A retained afterbirth is a very serious thing that can kill your doe. If the afterbirth is hanging part way out, and won't drop, you can tie a knot in the strands that are hanging to make more of a weight. If it is still hanging in 4 to 6 hours, call your veterinarian. Do not pull on it, or you could cause hemorrhaging.

Taking Care of the New Kids

The next order of business is keeping the new kids warm. Kids are very tough. You would be surprised what they can stand. However, they will do better if kept out of drafty areas, and if the temperature is under 30 degrees F, you should probably give them some extra heat for that first night. You can use a barn heater, or heat lamps. If you are going to use heat lamps – be careful! Position the heat lamp up high enough that the doe cannot scorch her fur by standing under it. Then tie it up securely by the handle and then separately by the cord. By sure that nothing flammable will come into contact with it, and make sure the bulb is screwed in tight. More barns are lost to heat lamp fires than any other accident. The next day, you can probably turn off the heat lamp during the day unless the temperature is under 20 degrees F, and then turn it back on at night. By the fourth day, kids that are nursing from their mothers should be weaned off supplementary heat completely unless your temperatures are under 20 degrees F.

Keep the new mother and her kids separate from the rest of the herd for at least three days so the kids will learn who mom is. Check them every two hours the first day to be sure they remember where dinner is kept, and then once a day after that for about the first week. (For more information on taking care of new kids, please see the next chapter, "Raising Kids".) A good mother will do the rest for you, and you have just enlarged your profit center!

Picture 26: A good mother will do the rest for you and you have just enlarged your profit center!*

Delivery Problems

What happens if things don't go as planned? What do you do if you go out to check on that mom that you saw wandering off by herself this morning, and she doesn't look right? What if she has been pushing for more than 30 minutes? It is for times like these that it is a very good idea to have a good veterinarian or experienced goat raiser, who lives within 15 minutes of your ranch, to call. Helping goats with difficult births is a skill and a gift. You have to have small hands, be able to think on your feet and <u>care about the animals</u>. If you don't have the gift, find someone who does. If your someone lives more than 15 minutes away, or can't be reached, here are some common sense solutions from my husband, David, who is not a veterinarian but is very good with goat delivery problems.

---

* This picture donated by Hill Country Farms from Spicewood, Texas.

What if the goat has been pushing for more than 30 minutes and nothing is coming out?

⇓Get someone to hold the goat's head for you. Put on a plastic or latex surgical glove that does not have powder on it. (According to veterinarians, the powder on latex gloves is very bad for the sensitive tissues involved in O.B. work.) Pour Betadine on the goat's vulva and then wipe it off with a paper towel. Pour Betadine on your gloved hand. Put some KY lubricant on your fingertips and put your hand in the goat's birth canal. You should be able to feel a little head, or tail or toes. Figure out what you are feeling, and then decide if this is a normal birth that is just taking a little longer, or if you have one of the problems described below. If the goat has been pushing for more than 60 minutes and you can't feel anything, get her to a veterinarian.

What happens if there are two hooves and no head?

You need to decide if you have front feet or back feet. If they are front feet, the toes will be pointed upwards and there will be a knee above the toes. If they are back feet, the toes will be pointed downwards and there will be a hock above the heel. If they are back feet, this is called a *breach birth*, put on plastic or latex surgical gloves and Betadine your hands. Pull gently on the feet in a downward motion, and they should come out easily. Be sure you have a tail coming next. Now remember that *a kid can breath through the umbilical cord until that cord breaks*, so you have time to work until the belly is born far enough to break the cord. If you have a tail coming next, gently help the doe to push the kid out by pulling when she pushes. Once the belly is born, then encourage the rest of the kid to slide out so that it can breath. Clear the mouth and the nose. If the kid seems to be having trouble breathing you can gently hold it by the back legs and the chest and swing it upside down to let the fluids drain out. This is actually considered a 'normal' birth.

⇓ PLEASE NOTE: I am not a veterinarian and have no veterinary training. It is not my intention to give medical advice. Before you follow any suggestion printed in this book that might be construed as medical advice, ALWAYS seek the advice of a qualified veterinarian.

If you have two front feet, and you can't find the head, then the head must be turned backwards. The kid can not be born this way. You must push the kid back into the mom far enough to find the nose and bring it forward with the feet. This requires a little time and some strong nerves. <u>Don't panic</u>. Call your experienced friend to start on their way over and go help the doe. She will cry. Push the kid back in, and feel along the shoulders for the head. Gently turn the head forward and guide the kid out with the head on top of the front legs. Clear the mouth and the nose. If the kid seems to be having trouble breathing you can gently hold it by the back legs and the chest and swing it upside down to let the fluids drain out.

What if there is one hoof and a nose?
If you only have one hoof and a nose presenting then the other hoof might be just a little bit back (just put your finger in a little ways where the hoof should be and feel for it). In which case everything will probably go just fine, or you may need to pull on it a little to get it together with the rest of the program. Or the missing hoof might be back along the body, or it might be folded up against the pelvic bone.

If the hoof is indeed missing, put a plastic or latex surgical glove on your hand and put Betadine on your glove. Feel along the kid's neck to the shoulder to try to decide if the leg is back along the body, or if it is folded up behind the pelvic bone. If the leg is truly missing, it is probably back along the body. Most does can kid in this position. Try helping the kid to ease forward. If it seems that it is going to come, then just continue to gently help the doe by pulling on the kid, in a downward motion, when she pushes.

ᵁIf the kid seems wedged, or the leg is folded up against the pelvic bone, you will have to push the kid back in and straighten out the leg. I would put a quick call in to my friend, and go back to help the doe. Put on a clean glove

---

ᵁ PLEASE NOTE: I am not a veterinarian and have no veterinary training. It is not my intention to give medical advice. Before you follow any suggestion printed in this book that might be construed as medical advice, ALWAYS seek the advice of a qualified veterinarian.

and some Betadine. Then push the kid back in. The doe will cry. Don't panic. Feel along the shoulder to find the missing leg. Be sure the leg you find belongs to this kid! Gently bring the leg forward, remembering how goat legs are hinged, until you can bring it up next to the other leg and help to guide the kid out with the nose on top of the front legs. Clear the mouth and the nose. If the kid seems to be having trouble breathing you can gently hold it by the back legs and the chest and swing it upside down to let the fluids drain out.

What if there is just a tail showing?
Very few does are large enough to kid this way. I did have one big old girl do it once, but that is pretty unusual. You need to put on your plastic or latex surgical gloves, wash the vulva with Betadine, then put Betadine on your glove. Then push the kid back in and follow the thighs down to find the rear legs, remembering how a goat is hinged, and gently bring the rear legs out first. Be absolutely sure that both legs you are pulling on actually belong to this kid! Then follow the directions above for a breach birth.

Note: If you have had to do an exam, or help your doe in one of the ways suggested above, you have just introduced germs into her delicate system – no matter how careful you have been! Many veterinarians suggest using an antibiotic bolus, intended for the purpose, to be inserted into the uterus. Some others may suggest an antibiotic by injection. Please call your veterinarian to see what he would have you do.

Moving Pregnant Goats

Any time you move goats to a new environment, you should take care that they don't become sick or have trouble with their rumen. Moving a pregnant goat should be done with even more attention to detail. A doe should not be moved during her last month of pregnancy unless absolutely necessary. A severe shock to her system can cause her to abort, or have trouble kidding. A pregnant doe should not be made to withstand being moved in a windy trailer, or being jostled around.

This holds true for handling a pregnant doe during normal ranching activities, as well. We once bought a doe that we did not realize was about to kid. She was in poor condition, and did not have that normal pregnant 'bloom' that she should have had. One of the first things we did was to put her on our hoof trimming table (like a calf table that tips the animal on their side) and fix her hooves. The next day she kidded with three bucks that were a tangled mess. If my husband was not very good at O.B. work, we would have lost them and their mother. Was this because we put her up on the table? I don't know, but I receive a lot of phone calls telling me about does that have been roughly handled near their kidding date, and then tried to deliver their kids in a jumble.

Kidding Kit or Bucket

It is a good idea to have a Kidding Kit or Bucket ready when you are expecting new arrivals. Even if you provide a minimum of assistance, it doesn't hurt to be prepared in case there is an emergency. Here is a list of some things to put into your kit:

➢   Plastic or latex, unpowdered, surgical gloves
➢   Umbilical clips (available from some animal products supply companies)
➢   Sharp scissors
➢   Dental floss
➢   7% Iodine
➢   Betadine
➢   Paper towels
➢   A chain and two sided clip in case you need to restrain the doe
➢   Packets of Gatoraide
➢   A bottle of one of the Goat Drench products that are out now containing propylene glycol
➢   Clean Newspapers
➢   Towels
➢   And it is always a good idea to have a lambing tube kit close by, just in case a kid is in need of instant nutrition.

Raising Kids

Raising kids for meat or breeding can be a rewarding and enjoyable project. Letting the natural mothers raise their kids can certainly facilitate this process. There are many good and valuable reasons to bottle feed kids. There are just as many reasons to let their mothers raise them. Personally, I leave the kids on the mothers if it is at all possible.

Does instinctively know when to feed their kids, and when to walk away. The few instances when does overfeed their kids almost always occur because the doe is a dairy goat who has been genetically engineered to give huge amounts of milk. We cannot blame the doe. However, most of the time, does do not over feed their kids, because they feed them small amounts at a time, and the milk is fresh and warm. Yes, there are times when the mother does not have enough milk, too. So you, as the breeder, should watch your kids and make sure that they are growing and thriving, and have fat little full bellies.

However, the instances of Enterotoxemia[43] [20] [21] or Coccidiosis, due to the management problems involved with bottle feeding, hugely outweigh the instances of milk related problems with kids who are raised on their natural mothers.   Enterotoxemia in kids occurs when the pH balance in their intestines suddenly changes.   This can be caused by a change in the milk that a kid is getting, as well as by a sudden increase in grain[43] [20].   Coccidiosis is caused by protozoal parasites that become a problem due to contamination of feed and water.   This is often a problem with young kids that are raised on a bottle because of the need to have them in a relatively confined, warm area.

Picture 27: Sometimes does seem to 'baby sit' for other moms in the herd .*

Raising Kids on Their Mother

I have covered this subject, to some extent, in the last chapter.   However, I feel that some things deserve to be restated.   When a new kid is born, you need to be sure that it gets colostrum within the first hour or so after birth.   Colostrum contains antibodies that will help your kids to fight off things like Enterotoxemia and Tetanus.

---

* This picture donated by Hill Country Farms from Spicewood, Texas.

Colostrum also contains sugars, fats and vitamins that will give your kids a good strong start.

Some kids just stand up and go find lunch all by themselves. Many, however, will do better to have a helping hand to get on a nipple the first time or two. The warm colostrum gives them a noticeable boost. You should clear the blockage that is usually present in the end of the teat, by milking the first few squirts from each teat into a cup or onto the straw. This will also clear a large percentage of the bacteria that is present in the end of the teat. After the kids have had their first good drink, I like to take a look every two hours or so the first day and make sure that the kids are getting up and remembering where to find dinner. If you go out once and the kids are sleeping, then go out again in two hours and the kids are sleeping, you need to stir them up and send them off toward mom.

You can tell if a kid's belly is full by putting your hand under his stomach and lifting up. Kids often have a lot of extra skin that makes them look thin even when they are not. When you lift up on him like this, you should be able to feel and see a firm, round full stomach. If you get a hand full of skin and air, your kid needs more to eat.

Many times a doe will not allow the kids to sleep too long. She will go and wake them up every little while. However, a weak kid will sometimes get too cold or 'sugared-out' to wake up and go get another boost of colostrum. In these cases, you will be glad that you took the time to check, because all that was needed was a little help to find the nipple one more time.

It is also a good practice to check the doe's udder the first day, and then in a day or two, to be sure that there are no lumps or sore spots. When you feel her udder, you should also milk out some milk to be sure that the milk flows easily, and there are no chunks or strings in the milk. Chunky or stringy milk, or lumpy udders, means mastitis. Many times it is only a very mild case and can be treated with an udder antibiotic preparation available in your local feed store. These preparations are, of course, made for cows so you should ask your veterinarian about dosages and frequency of treatments. If the milk will not flow without clogging, or the udder is hard and painful, you have a serious problem that requires the help of a veterinarian or experienced dairy goat breeder. However, if you had not checked, your kids would have died of starvation, and you would very likely have lost the mother as well. Good management requires a little more effort, but will pay off on sale day.

Keep new kids alone with their mother for three days, if you can. This makes a big difference to them when they do go out with the rest of the herd. They have had a little time to learn their mother's voice and smell, so they can find her around other goats. In fact, I tend to give them three days with mom, then put them out with two or three other new mothers, and their kids, for a few days. Then I will turn the whole bunch out into a private pen that can be opened onto the pasture, but close the gate for the night. Then I open the gate of the pen out onto the pasture the next day. This gives the new mothers and kids a 'base of operations' to run back to when it rains or gets dark.

Enterotoxemia in kids raised on their mother can occur when there is a change in the feed the kids are eating. This can happen when you change the grain ration you are giving the mother and she shares with her kids, or when the new grass comes up in the pasture and changes the pH balance in the mother's milk. The only way to be sure of preventing Enterotoxemia in kids on their mothers, is to vaccinate your newborns with C & D Perfringens antitoxin at birth. Then, you should vaccinate with C & D Perfringens toxoid at about three to four weeks old. Always be sure to watch for anaphylactic shock when giving C & D shots!

Raising Kids in Very Cold Weather

This subject is difficult to address because everyone's situation is so different. People that raise goats in the South, worry when the temperature gets below 50 degrees. And rightly so, because their goats are not used to it.

Goats are very adaptable. The most important thing to remember is that it is the *abnormal* weather that is dangerous for your goats.

However, new kids are born wet. Wet fur is very hard to dry in severe cold. Here in the Northwestern United States, we often kid out in weather that is about 20 degrees F and snowy. In weather like that, the kids need some warmth for the first few days. Not a lot, however. You can overdo a good thing. A spot in the pen that is a little warmer due to a barn heater or a heat lamp is usually enough. Also, when it is really cold, it helps to take some of the moisture out of the kid's fur with a blow dryer. I don't usually feel the need for a blow dryer down to about that 20 degree mark, but when the temperatures are below 20 degrees F - you just have to use your common sense.

Regardless of the temperatures, if the kids have a dry place to get out of the wet, and mothers to curl up with, they will probably do just fine after about the first week. Now, you can't just take them out of the barn and put them out in the blowing snow. Just like everything else, you have to do it gradually. The second day, turn off the heat lamp during the day and then put it back on at night. The third day, leave it off and see how you think they are doing. A cold kid will stand in the corner all humped up and shiver.

About the fifth day, try putting the doe and her kids out in a protected pen with a warm house, but block the kids into the house with a short board across one end. The seventh day you may be able to take the block out of the way and let them play in the pen. Etc. Your climate is different from mine. What works here may be ridiculous there. Watch for kids that are not bouncing around, or are hunched up and shivering. Listen for coughs and wheezing. Make sure they know their mothers and have fat little bellies. Use your common sense, pay attention to your goats, and you will do just great!

Raising Kids on a Bottle

There are many excellent reasons to raise kids on a bottle. There are several diseases that can be passed to the kids through nursing. If you are trying to eradicate these diseases from your ranch, bottle feeding, or surrogate mothers, may be your only option. Also, kids are more affectionate towards their human friends if they are bottle fed. It is easier to give medications and to know exactly how much milk a kid is getting if they are being bottle fed. If the mother gets sick or dies, you may be forced to bottle feed, or sell the kids at a discount to someone else who will.

Regardless of your reason, you now have a set of kids that you want to bottle feed. The first issue to deal with is colostrum. Kids must have colostrum to be healthy. If disease is not your reason for bottle feeding, you could milk some colostrum from the mother, or let the kids nurse for the first day or two. Researchers tell us that the kids only absorb the antibodies from colostrum for the first 12 to 24 hours. So the first day is the most important. However, there are also fats and sugars in colostrum that you will want to feed it, if you have it, for more than just the first day.

If disease is the issue, or the mother has mastitis or dies, you must find colostrum from another source. Many cattle ranches or dairies keep cow colostrum in the freezer at all times. If you are comfortable that their <u>cattle are not going to give your goats some unpleasant disease</u>, and you know someone who will sell some, this is a good option. However, do not be fooled, most diseases that you would be concerned with do <u>not die</u> in the freezer! Many ranchers keep colostrum, from the goats they know are healthy, in the freezer for emergencies. If you are good at planning ahead, this is definitely the best plan.

Another idea is the pre-packaged cow colostrum that you can buy at most feed stores. However, the fat in cow's milk has a different sized molecule than the fat in goat's milk. That is one reason why human babies have a harder time digesting cow's milk, and why goat kids will have a hard time with it too. Studies have shown that most colostrum substitutes are largely ineffective. The product that I finally decided worked the best for me, is a mix put out by the Meadow Mate company especially for goats. I have not seen any studies on this particular product, so I can't tell you if it is really better than the powdered substitutes, but it is the best I have found.

There is a new product, a "Goat Serum", developed from blood serum, which may alleviate the need for colostrum for our bottle fed kids.[19]

OK. Now you have your colostrum. Dry the kids off and give them about 4 ounces of colostrum (they will need at least 12 ounces of colostrum in the first 12 hours). I have found several nipples, but the ones that work for me, for newborns, are the red ones that are smaller and screw on to a pop bottle. Sometimes you have to work for a while to get the new kids to suck. *A tip: Goat mothers lick the kids' bottoms to stimulate sucking. If you can't get a kid to suck, set him in your lap, and try tickling him under his little tail with one hand while you hold the bottle in his mouth with the other.* Once they have had their bottle, put them in a box, with straw or a towel in the bottom. Put the box in a protected spot, but not where it will get too warm.

You cannot plan to keep the new kids in the house tonight and then put them out in a pen tomorrow, if it is at all cold outside. They do not have their mothers to keep them warm. Either they get to sleep in the laundry room until the weather warms up, or you will need to fix them up a protected spot in the barn with a source of heat.

Here is a feeding schedule that has worked for me in raising meat goats. (i.e.: Boers or Boer crosses) Each kid is an individual. Some kids require more or less milk than others. Do not assume that this schedule is right for your kids! Pay attention to how they act and what kind of condition they are in. Kids can get Enterotoxemia from bottle feeding when the pH balance in their intestines suddenly changes. This can happen if you suddenly change from natural milk to powdered milk, or if you suddenly change the amount of milk you are feeding. It can also happen if you suddenly start feeding grain to your bottle fed kids. All feeding changes should always be

made gradually! To prevent Enterotoxemia in your kids,
you should vaccinate with C & D Antitoxin at birth,
followed by C & D Perfringens toxoid at about 3 to 4 weeks
old.   Always be sure to watch for anaphylactic shock
when giving C & D shots!

New Born:	4 oz colostrum every 3 hours for the first 2 feedings.
Day One:	After the first 6 hours (above), feed 4 to 5 oz colostrum every 6 hours.
Day Two:	Feed 5 to 5 1/2 oz milk four times a day.
Day Three:	Feed 6 oz milk four times a day.
Day Four thru Nine:	Feed 9 oz milk four times a day.
Day Ten thru @ Day 20:	Feed 15 oz milk three times a day.
Day 21 thru 8-12 weeks:	Feed 20 oz milk three times a day.

Kids can be taught to drink from a 'lambing bar' or
caprine bucket.   This is a bucket with nipples which fit
into holes that have been drilled into the sides.   Tubes go
from the nipples into the bottom of the bucket.   The kids
suck on the nipples and the tubes work just like straws.
It can be a little difficult to get kids trained to use these
nipples, but you might try this: *Work with one or two kids
at a time. Put the milk into a tall, thin drinking glass and
then put the glasses into the bucket. 'Prime the pump' by
holding the end of the tube up in the air over the top of the
bucket. When the kid starts to suck, pour a little milk into
the tube. If the kid gets the idea, put the tube into the
glass. He will have an easier time with the glass because
the milk is in a narrower, taller space.* If you still want to
be sure how much each kid is getting after they are
trained, you can switch to quart jars in the bucket instead
of glasses.   One problem with this system is that the tubes
and nipples <u>must</u> be scrubbed out, thoroughly, every day.

I provide fine-stemmed hay for my meat kids starting
about the 2nd day.   Most meat kids are eating by the end
of the first week.   You should also provide your young kids
with a small bowl of your creep feed, and a small bowl of
fresh water, after the first week.

Picture 28: Kids on a 'lamb bar' or 'caprine bucket'.[*]

If your bottle fed kids get black sticky diarrhea, after the first 24 hours, please read the section about Coccidiosis in the "Health Needs and Potential Problems" chapter of this book.

Grafting Kids onto Surrogate Mothers

A surrogate mother is a doe who is not the kid's natural mother. When you do an embryo transfer program the recipient does are called surrogates. You may also want to graft a kid onto a surrogate mother if you have an orphaned kid or kids, for whatever reason, and you want to give them a new mom. Many people say this cannot be done. I do it every year. It takes persistence, common sense and a doe with good mothering instincts.

---

[*] This picture donated by Golden Haze Farm from Calgary, Alberta Canada.

I learned how to graft kids onto new mothers when I had a weak triplet born one year. The mother was a first time kidder and had two big kids and one tiny 3 pound doeling. We took the little one into the house and nursed her by hand for the first two weeks, then were ready to turn the job over to someone else. But who, and how? The following methods have both worked for me whenever I have kids that need more milk than their mother can give them, the mother was sick or has had too many kids to care for.

You need a doe who is just kidding, or has kidded within the last three weeks. I don't think even Method 2 below would work after three weeks unless you have a 'nurse goat' (A nurse goat is a doe who will mother anything. These does are usually hard to have around, because they don't get along with other goats very well, but if you discover you have one, you may find she is worth the trouble.) This means that you have to plan the graft ahead of time. You need to do something with the doe's natural kids. Sometimes it will work if you let her keep one of her kids, but it is easier if you deprive her of both of her own kids. Maybe she only had one, and you know she will have enough milk for two, and another doe just had three. Maybe you have her kids pre-sold (This happens to me a lot because I sell Boer cross kids for pack goats at four days old.) Maybe the kids you want to graft are worth enough to you that you will sell the doe's natural kids to someone at a severe discount to bottle raise. However you do it, you need a doe who has just kidded.

Method 1: The graft will be easier if you can arrange to feed some of the surrogate mother's milk to the kids for two days before the graft. It takes about 48 hours for a mother's milk to get all the way through the kid, and make it smell like her kids. Sometimes you can milk out small amounts of a doe's colostrum one or two days before she kids. The problem with this is that she may not have any colostrum for her natural kids by the time she actually kids. This is up to you, and may not even be possible, but in extreme situations, it may be worth a try. Have the replacement kids there when the surrogate mother begins her delivery. Put one of the kids to be grafted behind the doe as she kids and try to confuse it with her natural kid by covering it with the afterbirth and the doe's blood. Occasionally, this will just work and she won't know it isn't her kid, especially if her natural kids have been wisked away before she can smell them. Of course, the kid knows that this isn't his mom, so you will still need to go out every few hours and show him where dinner is now kept until he gets it figured out.

Method 2: If the above doesn't work, or you can't be there with the new family during kidding, or feed the kid the new mother's milk for three days before she kids, the following will usually work. Tie the doe in a small pen (about 8 or ten feet square), on about a 6 foot leash. Be sure she can eat and drink and lay down. Try to be sure she can't strangle herself by getting caught around a feeder or something. This short leash will allow the kids to stay out of her way, and she won't be able to chase them. Now, arrange another chain so that you can tie her collar directly to the fence, so she can't move at all. You might even need to have another tie to go around her middle to keep her from kicking away from you when you are working with her new kids. Take her natural kids away from her and sell them to that breeder who wants to bottle feed.

Now you are ready to bring her the new kids. Tie her up tight so she can't move (don't forget to be gentle, you don't want her to associate these kids with being handled too roughly). Bring the kids out and try to get them to drink. This may be harder than you think, because they don't associate this doe with food. However, don't give up. Squirt some milk in their mouths, put them on the nipple and just gently hold them there. Usually they get the idea and start sucking. If not, try again later. Kids have an incredible survival instinct and will pretty much eat when they get hungry, unless they get too weak. When the kids have had a drink, put them behind her and turn her loose on her 6 foot leash. Stay for a while to make sure she doesn't hurt the kids. Be sure they can get to a place behind her where she can't reach them. If they are too young to understand this, block them into the section of the pen where they will be safe with a piece of board (I have used this method with kids that are two days old all the way to three weeks old). Don't take the kids back into

the house. They have to get used to being with this doe,
even if they aren't touching her.

Then, in two hours, try to get the kids to nurse again.
Sometimes the kids will seem to get the idea, and later
they will seem to have forgotten. Don't give up. Keep
going out four times a day, and putting those kids on the
nipple. Don't give them any other doe's milk! By the third
day, they will be running to a nipple when they see you
coming to hold the doe. However, it often takes longer
than three days for her to let them nurse when she is
alone with them. I don't turn her loose with them in the
small pen. I usually take them to a larger area, once the
kids will <u>always</u> come to nurse when they see me coming,
where they are still confined, but the kids can get away
from the doe if she decides to chase them.

Keep going out four times a day and catching the doe for
the kids to nurse. In about two weeks, you will notice that
she just stops when she sees you coming, and the kids
will run to nurse. If you walk away, she may kick them
away, so just stand there as though you were holding her.
Then, one day, you will see the kids nursing when she is
eating. Eventually, she will just forget they aren't hers. If
you want to speed things up, try putting another doe and
her kids in with them after about the first three weeks.
Sometimes the doe will claim the kids faster because she
feels protective of them around another doe.

Yes, this is a long process, but if you don't want to bottle
feed, and you only have one set of kids to deal with, it can
be a good alternative.

Creep Feeding your Kids

Whether you are bottle feeding, letting the does raise their
kids, raising breeding stock or raising meat stock, creep
feeding your kids is essential. Kids cannot compete with
adult goats for the choicer feeds that they need to grow to
their fullest potential. It may be true that the kids walk all
over your feeders and the mothers may get out of their

way, but they are not really getting the kinds of feed that you can give them in a creep.

A creep is a place that the kids can get into but the adult goats cannot. It can be a specially factory made system of fencing panels with kid sized holes in one side, or something homemade. Remember the calf houses that we use in our kidding pens? Well, to use them for kidding pens we had to take the front panels off that have the holes in them for the calves to put their heads through to eat. Some of our creeps are constructed of three plywood sides, and one of these calf panels on the forth side. One of our creeps has an old wooden gate for the forth side that has wide enough holes between the slats to let a kid through. Creeps only need to be big enough to accommodate the kids that will be using them. 4 foot by 4 foot creep will work if you only have a few kids. One of our creeps opens onto a special enclosed yard where the goat kids and my kids can play together without their mothers interfering.

Inside the creep should be a kid sized hay rack, and a bowl of creep pellets. Several companies sell one-flake hay racks for traveling that cost about $10.00. These work well in a creep when they are screwed to the wall with the bottom of the rack about 18 inches from the ground. (If you put the rack too close to the ground, the kids may climb into it and get stuck!) Creep pellets can be any kind of high protein (about 10-18%) pellets that are made for kids. Several companies make pellets specifically for this purpose. I use my standard goat pellet plus a top dressing of 'milk pellets'. These are high protein and vitamin pellets that are specially made for young animals.

How to Care for Weak Kids

About once a year we have a kid born that inhaled too much mucous, or just can't seem to get going, or has gotten chilled before we found it. The first thing to do when you find a kid that you think might be in trouble is put your finger in its mouth. The normal body temperature for goats is higher than yours, so their mouths should feel warm. If the mouth is cool, the kid is

Picture 29: A creep is any place a kid can get into but the adult goats can't.[*]

chilled or sick.   It is a good idea to involve your veterinarian when you have weak kids.   They see a lot more of them than you are likely to, and will have instruments and drugs to improve your kid's chances. However, the vet is not always available, so here are some ideas to try until he can be reached.

What can you do if a kid was born breach, the bag was on too long, or for whatever reason, it has inhaled fluids? Pick the kid up by the back legs, support it by its chest, and swing it gently between your legs. This will help the fluid to drain out of the nose and mouth. Some people use a human baby bulb syringe, but I have never gotten it to work. Get as much fluid out as possible.

If the kid is too weak to suck, you can give it about 1cc of 50% Dextrose on the tongue (You can buy 50% Dextrose at your feed store.   Draw 1cc out with a syringe and

[*] This picture donated by Hill Country Farms from Spicewood, Texas.

needle, then take off the needle and slowly put the Dextrose in the kid's mouth.) This will give it a boost. If it is still too weak to suck you may have to put a tube into its stomach to give it a little colostrum.

Tubing a kid is a learned skill, and it would help if you have someone show you how the first several times. If you are on your own, this is how it is done: You need a 'lambing tube'. This is a small stomach tube and a large syringe that fits into one end of the tube. It is a good idea to hold the tube up to the kid's body and estimate the distance from the kid's mouth to its stomach. Mark this distance on the tube, so you have an idea how far to put the tube in.

You want to put the tube down the left side of the kid's throat. So you open the kid's mouth, put your finger in to keep it open, put the tube in its mouth on the right side and go across the tongue to the kid's left side of the throat. Push the tube gently in. If you tip the kid's head up, you should be able to see and feel the tube going down. If you cannot see or feel it, and if the kid is breathing through it, pull it back out and try again. Also, the distance from the mouth to the lungs is a lot less than from the mouth to the stomach. Once you are sure you have the tube in the right place, put the syringe in the end you are holding and give it 2 to 3 ounces of warm colostrum. This procedure saves many kids that are just a little too weak to get started on their own.

If the kid has gotten too cold before you found it, you must take it inside and warm it up! Put it in your coat, and take it inside. Try giving it some Dextrose and some warm colostrum. If it is very cold you can submerge it's body in warm (100 degree F) water, being careful not to get the nose wet. Then dry it off carefully and, if you haven't already, get some Dextrose and Colostrum into it. As soon as it is dry and active you need to try to get it back to mom or she may not want to take it.

Always listen to your new kids every couple of days. I even bought a stethoscope for this purpose. If they are wheezing, you need to ask your veterinarian about giving them a little penicillin to be sure they don't have a slight lung infection from inhaling too many fluids during birth.

Floppy Kid Syndrome

Floppy Kid Syndrome is a poorly understood disease that can attack a barn and kill high percentages of kids. Here in the Northwestern United States we don't see the real thing, but occasionally I will have a kid that has been doing just fine, and suddenly doesn't want to get up. I give it a little penicillin (after checking with my veterinarian) and some Dextrose, and it usually pops right back up. Is that a mild case? Probably not, I don't know, but here is a good explanation of what to do for the real thing:

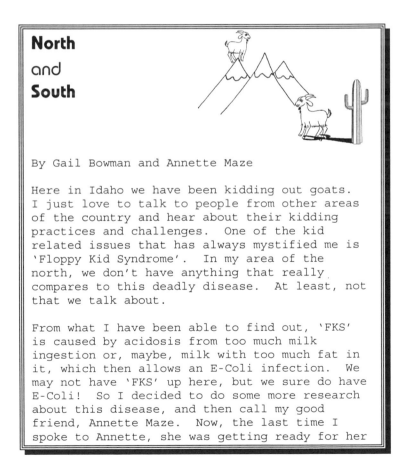

North and South

By Gail Bowman and Annette Maze

Here in Idaho we have been kidding out goats. I just love to talk to people from other areas of the country and hear about their kidding practices and challenges. One of the kid related issues that has always mystified me is 'Floppy Kid Syndrome'. In my area of the north, we don't have anything that really compares to this deadly disease. At least, not that we talk about.

From what I have been able to find out, 'FKS' is caused by acidosis from too much milk ingestion or, maybe, milk with too much fat in it, which then allows an E-Coli infection. We may not have 'FKS' up here, but we sure do have E-Coli! So I decided to do some more research about this disease, and then call my good friend, Annette Maze. Now, the last time I spoke to Annette, she was getting ready for her

big trip to South Africa to attend the South
African National Boer Goat Show. I wonder how
that went. Would you like to listen in?

"Hello-o"

"Hi there! It's me, Gail"

"Yes ma-um, what can I do for you?"

"Well, I was wondering how your trip to
Africa went."

"Well, I saw some wonderful goats, and went
to a very informative goat show, met a lot of
very exciting goat ranchers, and I did some
real fun shopping!"

"Shopping! Like for jewelry, or what?"

"Well, Honey, I could have shopped for all
the jewelry I wanted! But I just wasn't
prepared to have that much fun. No, I bought a
beautiful ostrich brief case! You just would
not believe the fabulous leather products over
there!"

"Well, the next time you, like, wander off
to Africa, especially if there's shopping to be
done, put me in your suit case. OK?"

"Yes ma-um."

"Hey, Annette, I've been trying to figure
out this 'Floppy Kid Syndrome' thing."

"Yes ma-um."

"I'm reading some articles by Andres de la
Concha and Fred Homeyer.[22] [23] And, like, they
are saying that it seems to be too much milk,
or too much fat in the milk, where the milk
seems to go bad in the kid's tummy and cause
acidosis, which then leads to systemic
infection by E-Coli. But it seems that it is
only kids that are penned up in a confined
area. Have you found that to be true?"

"No ma um. I have seen it in kids that
have not been in a small, confined area. These
kids are getting inferior colostrum. For some
reason, there are not enough antibodies in the
colostrum. And it does not necessarily hit
both twins, and it will not necessarily be
contagious. But it hits the kids at two to
three days old."

"Oh, so this isn't something that hits,
like, the first day."

"No ma-um, it's usually two to three days
old. And there is always a high incidence of
E-Coli. But don't let down your guard just

because the kids are 3 days old! 'FKS' can
still hit any time up until the kids are 21
days old!"

"Well, like, how do you know when it
starts? Do you just go out and find the kids
collapsed on the ground?"

"Not if you are watching your kids. If you
are watching your kids you will see a little
bit of a hitch in their get-a-long."

"Excuse me? I don't think we have "get-a-
longs" here in Idaho!"

"Well honey, that is your loss! Here in
Texas we are very proud of our "get-a-longs",
let me tell you! What I mean is, that they
will be walking and they will kinda go like
they're drunk, two, three, four. And then they
will seem to be all right, and then they will
just seem to drag their back legs."

"Do you think that 'FKS' is more prevalent
in the south because of the warmer
temperatures?"

"Yes ma-um. The mortality rate goes
higher, the warmer it gets."

"And, then to treat it, Dr. de la Concha
says in his article "Finding a cure for
'Floppy' Kid Syndrome" that the first thing to
do is to neutralize the acidosis by giving the
kids "between 20 and 50 mls (cc's) of a
solution, made by dissolving a spoon of sodium
bicarbonate (baking soda) in a glass of water,
orally with a syringe. Do it slowly so the kid
has time to swallow. Repeat the treatment at
1, 3, 6 and 12 hours as needed. The most
crucial thing is to keep kids off milk for
approximately 24 hours." Have you found that
that works?"

"Yes ma-um. And if they are too weak to
swallow, you have to get it in them by using a
lambing tube. Then, what does Dr. de la Concha
say to give them for the E-Coli?"

"He says to give "A single shot of
oxytetracycline intramuscularly.""

"Yes ma-um. You must get an anti-infective
in there to neutralize the E-Coli."

"Well, I had better, like, tell people to
<u>always check with their veterinarian before</u>
<u>they administer any drug</u> to their goats! But

> that is the one that works for you? Well,
> I'm sure that people will be happy to have a
> specific drug to ask their Vets about when they
> ask about treating this disease."
>
> "Yes ma-um. You are very lucky that you
> don't get it up there in the frozen wastes!"♥

Tattooing, Tagging and Micro Chips

Whether you are raising kids for meat production or breeding stock, it is important to be able to identify who is who and know when they were born. If you are raising 600 meat goats, you probably don't tag the kids that you know will be going to the sale in 3 months, unless you need to know which ones go to which sale. Never the less, you will still need to identify the does you decide to keep for replacement stock.

I have found ear tagging to be the easiest form of identification. It is fast, reliable, can be easily changed if you change your mind, and ear tags are available in a huge assortment of shapes, sizes and colors. I use a different color tag for different percentages of Boer blood. My friend uses a different tag for different birth months, or different E. T. mothers. However, ear tags are not permanent identification. Simply because they are easy to change, they can break or rip out, and after years of wear, the numbers can wear off.

I have dog collars on all my goats because I don't have very many, and it makes them easier to handle. Last year, when two of my goats ripped their ear tags out in freak accidents, I decided to change all my breeding stock tags to neck tags. However, neck tags are a lot easier to lose, and permanent collars on bucks can be a hazard when they start to play. One young buck almost died the other day, when another buck hooked his horn through his collar and became tangled.

♥ This 'North and South' appeared in <u>The Goat Rancher Magazine</u> in May 1997

Tattooing is a permanent, inexpensive means of identifying your animals. True, tattoos cannot be read from across the pasture, but they don't rip out, rub off or get tangled in someone's horns. I suggest a combination of either neck or ear tags, and tattooing. To give a good tattoo, you will need a tattoo kit, some green paste type ink, a tooth brush and some baking soda. Begin by cleaning the ear with an alcohol wipe, then brushing some ink on the ear in the open space that is in the center of the ear, between the cartilage and the veins. Holding the ear out at an acute angle from the goat's head, bring the tattoo pliers up from the bottom of the ear with the needles on the inside of the ear. Close the pliers with a quick, firm movement, and then carefully remove the pliers. Immediately apply more ink with the toothbrush and continue rubbing it in for at least 15 seconds. The baking soda is to press into the tattoo after you are done. I have found that this helps to stop any bleeding and allows less ink to get on the goat's fur. Now you need to leave the tattoo alone until it is healed.

Microchips are permanent but much more expensive. You also need a special reader to read them. Very few people do their own microchipping, although the process is not difficult. If you are interested in this means of identifying your goats, I suggest you discuss it with your veterinarian.

Weaning Kids and Drying off Moms

At what age to wean your kids is another subject of wide discussion. You will hear everything from 8 weeks to 5 months. Many people wean their kids at 8 weeks because it allows the mothers to recover and rebreed sooner. Another reason to wean early is because the buck kids can get so strong that they damage their mother's udders when they nurse. Some people have even told me that their kids grow faster if they can get them on totally solid feed sooner. I have not found this last reason to hold true on my ranch.

I have found that kids left on their mothers for a longer time grow faster. I still creep feed the kids, even while they are nursing, so there is really no reason that they would not benefit from the extra nutrition. For this reason, I leave my breeding stock kids on their mothers at least 12 weeks. Then I remove the bucks and put them in a separate pen as far away from the mothers as possible. I tend to leave the doelings with their mothers for 14 to16 weeks. However, if the doe is a heavy milker, it doesn't work to take her buck away and just leave her doeling with her, because the doeling will either get too much milk, or only nurse from one side allowing the other side to get mastitis.

You must make decisions on weaning times that work for you. Sometimes, a kid will be weaned because all the rest of the kids are due to be weaned at that time, even if it is a little early or late for that kid. Often a kid is weaned at a certain time because they have been sold. Be careful about taking a kid directly away from its mother and moving it to another ranch. Many times the kid will be fine, and will not have the trauma of crying for mom, because mom isn't there to answer. However, occasionally, a kid will have <u>more</u> trouble with the move because of the double trauma of being weaned.

Once you have moved the kids away from their mothers, they will do better if they cannot reach mom through a fence, and mom will be more likely to get on with her life if she cannot nuzzle her kids. No matter what you do, if they can hear each other cry, you will have several days of noise to endure. For this reason, I try to wean kids in groups, about twice or three times a year.

Now you need to dry off the mothers. When I first started raising goats, I asked my veterinarian whether I should try to dry off the does by milking less frequently. He said that I should just not milk them. Period. Put them somewhere that they have no access to any feed except hay and water. No grain at all. And let them be miserable for a few weeks. The pressure of the milk will cause the glands to stop producing and the body will eventually reabsorb the extra milk.

Picture 30: A Fainting Goat doe and her kid.[*]

This works perfectly for most <u>meat</u> goats. However, again, dairy goats have been genetically engineered for a thousand years to give lots of milk. Occasionally, this method even works for dairy goats. However, <u>most dairy goats</u>, and dairy-meat crosses, just cannot dry off this way. If you have one of these does, as I do, I suggest that you learn to milk, or enlist the advice of a very knowledgeable dairy breeder. Because dairy goats were just not intended to be dried off before they have finished their natural cycle. Once you have had a doe with serious mastitis, you will never want to do it again.

Castrating

One mature buck can breed at least 50 does a year. Yet, half the kids born are male. This is where we get our meat crop. Bucks that have been castrated are called wethers. Wethers and surplus, or flawed, does are the cash crop that we are in this business to raise. For meat.

---

[*] This picture donated by Phil Sponenburg from Blacksburg, Virginia.

A buck that has been castrated will not grow as fast as one that has not been castrated. If you are raising meat, you will probably want to castrate after the kid has had some time to put on some growth. If you are castrating to make a buck into a pet, you need to consider that the urethra will quit growing when the buck is castrated. The older you castrate a buck for a pet, the better chance he will have of escaping urinary calculi disease. Because of the growth issue, I prefer to wait to castrate my meat bucks until they are 6 weeks old. Any older and the testicles are almost too big to work with.

There are several ways to castrate a buck. There is a tool called an emasculator, or Burdizzo. If you are castrating for meat, and the wether will not be running with the does in your herd, this method might work for you. Using this special tool, you can crush the cords to the testicles, hopefully, making the buck into a wether.

You can castrate with a knife. You cut the bottom end off the scrotum, pull out the testicles, and with a shaving motion of your knife, 'fray' them off. There will be quite a lot of bleating and occasionally, you can get one that bleeds. Veterinarians may tell you that this method heals the most quickly and is the most humane. Always be sure to use an antibiotic spray and a screw worm spray.

You can also 'band' them. With a special tool called an elastrator, you can put a small rubber band (manufactured for the purpose) carefully above the testicles. Be sure that you have both testicles below the band! Some people say that this method is inhumane. I don't agree. The bucks will lay around and be very uncomfortable for about a day, then everything goes numb and they are back to normal. One problem with using this method on goats is that goats have such a lot of sheer mass in that part of their anatomy. For this reason, you may want to band the animals that you know are going for meat, at about 3 to 7 days old.

Sometimes the testicles can get infected before they have a chance to fall off, especially if you have waited until the buck is older to castrate him. So I go back to the wether 5 days after he has been banded, and carefully cut off the dead tissue <u>below</u> the band. You want to leave the band and about ¼ inch of skin below it, but you can cut off the rest with a sharp pair of scissors. This does not hurt the wether, unless you pull on him as you go. There will be no blood. The remaining skin sort of 'flowers' out around the band and the whole thing will come off as one big scab in about 6 weeks. I always put an antiseptic spray and a screw worm spray on it when I cut off the extra flesh, and again when the scab comes off.

Dehorning or Disbudding

Dehorning or Disbudding your goats is a personal choice. In general, meat breeders do not disbud their goats because goats were intended to have horns. There is some evidence that goats exchange heat through the blood flow in their horns. This would mean that goats will actually withstand extreme weather conditions better if their horns are left intact. In any case, goats are certainly more able to defend themselves against predators if they have horns.

However, many breeders prefer to follow the dairy tradition of disbudding. There are many reasons, all of them worthwhile. Probably the best reason to disbud is so the goat will not be as likely to get caught in a fence, or injure another goat. Also, dairy goat ranchers have to milk their goats twice a day, every day. They have a lot more opportunity to get caught by a goat's horns themselves than a meat raiser who only handles his animals to give vaccinations, trim hooves, and possibly help kid. Also, dairy goats are typically housed in much closer quarters, often a barn or small pens, while meat goats are usually allowed to roam large pastures or acreages. Dairy goats are not as exposed to the dangers of depredation, by dogs or coyotes, as meat goats are, so they have no need to defend themselves. I do not dehorn or disbud my goats but, as I said, the choice is entirely individual.

If you do decide to disbud, the process is only "disbudding" before the kid is one week old. After that, it is "dehorning". Goats have a much greater blood flow and deeper attachment in their horns than cattle do. While dehorning an adult cow is a reasonably simple task, it is life threatening to a goat. There are several different methods of disbudding, the most effective and humane in my experience, is to burn the "bud" with a hot iron before the kid is 7 days old. There is more risk of side effects from anesthesia than there are from disbudding without anesthesia, but it requires experience and a strong stomach. I strongly recommend that you enlist the help of an experienced veterinarian or dairy goat breeder to teach you this skill!

NOTES:

NOTES:

Marketing your Goats

It doesn't matter in the least if you have the most fabulous goats in the world, and they have each kidded with triplets, and the kids are all growing like crazy, if you have no place to sell your goats. No one can buy your goats if you sit on the ranch and whine about not selling any goats! You would be surprised how many people call me and tell me that they can't sell their goats. When I ask them if they have done any advertising, or sent out any flyers, or put their goats in any kind of exhibition, the phone just goes dead.

If you are going to raise livestock to sell, you need to figure out a way to sell it. If you are raising meat goats, you need to tap into some of the direct market niches discussed in Chapter 2, or find a good sale to ship your goats to. If you are raising breeding stock, you need to advertise. As a dear friend of mine is fond of saying, "No one can buy your goats if they don't know you are there!"

Try Telling the Truth

In my experience, the very most important ingredient to increased future sales is telling the truth the first time around! Your best sales contacts will be by word of mouth. This is true even if the buyer lives across the continent from you. If you tell someone that a goat is something that it isn't, or that it is not something that it turns out to be, you have just shot yourself in the foot. That person will eventually find out that you lied. He will be mad – for years! He will tell everyone that he meets what a rotten deal you gave him, and the deal will get worse every time he tells it. This kind of publicity knows no geographic or temporal bounds. You <u>do not</u> want to go there.

However, you can still sell animals that have certain types of problems. You will have buyers come to you that want a great deal. If you carefully explain to this person that this animal has this problem, whether it is a flaw or an illness, someone will want that animal at a good enough discount. Then, when that person gets three years down the road, and discovers that they really do care about that defect, they have no reason to be mad at you. You pointed it out to start with. I am amazed at how true this is.

You can also sell that animal at the auction yards. People who buy animals at these facilities should be aware that the animals might have problems. However, if the problem is sterility, or a disease that is contagious, the animal should be killed. It is not honest marketing, even at an auction yard, to sell animals that you know will not breed, or that might spread disease to unsuspecting buyers.

Identify your Market

The first thing to establish is, "What are you trying to sell?" If you are trying to sell goats for meat, take the following steps to establish a direct market for your goats:

✓ Call the dairy goat breeders in your area and ask if there is someone, or some group, in the area that they sell their wethers to. Most of them have such a group, if they will share the information with you.

✓ Put an ad in several local newspapers, in the early spring, that reads something like this:

> Meat goats for sale. Good 4-H projects or perfect for the barbecue. Call:

✓ Take a tour of the yellow pages and see if there are any restaurants in your area that serve authentic Greek, Mexican, Asian, African, or Caribbean cuisine. Give these a call and find out if they would be interested in high quality goat meat, and what you would have to do to be able to sell to them. Will they arrange to butcher their own? Would they like a whole loin as a sample? How much would they pay? One Greek restaurant I spoke to was willing to pay $4.50 a pound, but only wanted certain cuts.

✓ If your kids are good enough to be used as breeding stock, advertise in the newspaper that you have meat goat breeding stock for sale. A different group of people will call in response to this ad.

✓ Check out the sale yards in your area. Do they sell goats? How much do they sell for? Call around. Many times, it is worth a drive to go to a sale that brings a better price.

✓ Ask other breeders if there are any cooperatives or meat goat associations near by. Get involved.

If you are primarily trying to sell breeding stock:

✓ Find out if there are herds of meat goats in the area. These breeders are often interested in new stock.

✓ Check with the registry associations and see if they have a contact person for your area.

✓ Start getting involved with other breeders. Go to shows.

✓ Find out if your local fair will allow you to bring your goats for an exhibition.

✓ Make a list of the dairy goat breeders in your area, and send them a flyer about your meat goats. You might be surprised at the response you will get.

✓ Make phone calls to breeders of goats. Any kind of goats. All they can do is tell you you're crazy. Make contact.

✓ Identify fullblood breeders – anywhere. Call them, send them flyers, go to see them, develop a relationship.

✓ Be a good host. Hold a free goat barbecue (Check out my recipe, 'Seminar Barbecue'), and invite your dairy goat friends and your neighbors, and ask them to bring their rancher friends.

✓ Ask the meat goat registry associations if you can host a seminar or workshop on your ranch.

✓ When that rancher down the street asks you what 'them things' taste like, hand him a package of chevon steaks!

Ranching For Sales

What will you do if someone actually shows up at your ranch? You will have to take them out to see your goats. Go out and take the same tour yourself, with a stranger's eyes. What do you see? Is there junk laying around? Are last year's tires, and the year's before that, laying in the walkway because you were going to make flower pots? What about old wire and baling twine? In fact, does your ranch look like a junk yard?

What about the goats? Are they well fed? Do you have the sick ones housed in the first pen, so they are the first impression people are going to get? What does the water look like? Are you feeding on the ground? That's right, go out and take a good look at your ranch.

Now consider this; would you buy your goats? No one has a perfect ranch. Part of ranching is the accumulation of junk. However, it could be stored behind the barn. And animals will get sick, but you should have a sick pen that is out of the way, where you can keep people away from it. Reread Chapter 4 on buying goats, and apply that same advice to your own ranch.

If your ranch looks good, and you sound like you know what you are doing, and your animals look great, you will make sales.

Showing your Goats

If you have show-worthy goats, and you like to show, showing your goats can be a tremendous sales tool. Think about it. The people that come to goat shows are either breeders, or prospective breeders who are interested in your specific breed. I would advise anyone who likes to play the 'showing game' to take two or three of their best goats to at least one goat show a year.

Do not take goats that have just kidded, or are in poor condition to a show. You want to take goats that are well fleshed, and have been grained for a month or so before the show, so they are shiny and a little plump. Fat goats are not a good thing, even at shows, but thin goats show incredibly badly, and would be better off left at home.

When I am getting ready for a show, I choose the goats that I think have the best body type and conformation. Then I make sure that they are going to be in the right physical condition by the time of the show. You want to take kids that are over 6 weeks old, does that are two or three months pregnant, bucks that are in their prime and up on their pasterns, does who have kidded at least 6 weeks ago and have regained their 'figure', etc. It is very risky to take a doe who is in her last six weeks of pregnancy. You do not want a doe who just kidded and looks like she hasn't eaten in a year, or a doe who has milked away all her body fat. You do not want a buck who can not stand up on his feet and legs well, or who is too thin. Tiny, new kids are seldom an asset.

Bring the goats that you have decided to show into a separate area, about a month before the show. If they are not tame, or accustomed to being led on a leash, you can tame them this way:
♦ Put them into a small pen all alone. A goat that is lonely will tame down much faster than a goat who has friends to talk to.

♦ Go out and see each goat for several minutes, three times a day.

♦ The first day, bring her a little grain or a treat every time you go to see her.

♦ The second day, chain her up on a short chain (about 12 to 18 inches long) for a few minutes during the time you are out with her, and give her a treat while she is on the chain.

♦ The third day, pet her while she is on her chain and is eating her treat.

♦ The forth day, pet her and feed her while she is on the chain, then leave her on it for 15 minutes without you.

♦ Continue in this way until the goat is not afraid of being on a chain, and will let you pet and brush her all over her body. You need to touch her udder when you are petting her, because the judge will.

♦ After a week and a half or two weeks of working on a chain, try taking her for a short walk (15 feet) before she gets her treat.

♦ Lengthen the walk a little every day until the goat is comfortable walking everywhere with you. You should spend a lot of time (at least an hour a day) walking each goat, so they are comfortable on a leash.

Now you have your show goats leash trained. The day before the show, or before you have to leave for the show, you should wash your goats with a good animal shampoo, then use a spray conditioner. Brush out any undercoat that might be hanging on, unless it is the middle of winter. Be careful washing your goats if it is too cold and you have to travel. You might be better off washing them at the show site, than making them sick by washing them, and then getting them chilled.

My friend and I wrote a North and South about showing goats, I think you will enjoy it:

North
And
South

By Gail Bowman and Annette Maze

I just returned from showing my goats in my
first real goat show. What an experience!
When I was talking to my neighbor about it, he
told me a little story that I just couldn't
wait to share with my friend Annette Maze!
Let's give her a call.

"Hello-o."
"Hi there! This is Gail!"
"Yes ma-um, what can I do for you?"
"Well, I have a new goat joke for you."
"Well honey, let me have it!"
"OK. I was complaining to my Texan
neighbor that I was trying to teach my 350
pound Boer buck to lead for a goat show. And
every time I tried to get him to lead in a
clockwise direction, like they say to do you
know, he would insist on turning the other way.
My neighbor said he had just the same problem
with an old horse he was trying to train. He
said that every time he tried to get him to
turn left, he would insist on turning right."
"So what did he do?"
"Well, he said he just put a little piece
of lead in the horse's right ear."
"Really? And that worked? Well how did he
get it to stay in there?"
"He said he just used a little old 22
pistol."
"Ahh! Well Honey, I happen to know what
you paid for that 350 pound buck, and I don't
suggest you use that particular method."
"Well, I could always employ the method
that my husband, David, used to keep the little
buck kid in line that he was showing last
week."
"Yes Ma-um. I'm almost afraid to ask."
"Well, he just kinda let the little guy
chew on his beard."

"Are you aware that there is a correct way to show a goat?"

"No! Really! Well, for one thing, how do you get them to follow you out into the ring?"

"It's actually pretty easy if you train them before they get to be 350 pounds! Most people start training their goats to lead when they are tiny kids. Breeders have also been known to pet and brush their little goats to get them used to being touched. However, I can navigate even a 350 pound buck with a collar called a 'German choke chain'. It can be purchased at any large pet store. They come in many sizes."

"Really? Like, I have never even heard of that!"

"Usually, when a show animal drags you around the ring a few times you will try anything. The most common mistake an exhibitor makes is to allow the lead chain to slide down the neck. You hold the most leverage when the lead is right under the back of the jaw. Also, some exhibitors just jerk their goats out of the pens and hurry right into the ring. This upsets the animal. I have my helper walk each animal a short distance before I take it out into the ring."

"That is, like really great advice! But what about the rumblings I have been hearing about letting animals loose in the ring?"

"Yes ma-um. There are just lots of answers to that question. It can be helpful for a judge to see free movement of the animals side by side. However, one must have excellent fences around the ring, closed gates that stay closed, and exhibitors that don't mind doing a lot of running and catching. I recently watched the South African National Show. There were 84 handlers chasing after 84 little Boer does. The entertainment value was definitely better than some of our more reserved shows here in the states."

"Wow! Cool! I think that would be a great way to show goats! No chain collars, no staying on the other side from the judge, just turn 'em loose!"

"Yes Ma-um. And I would probably consider letting the top 6 loose, but more than that could be called a rodeo rather than a show!

Excellent quality Boer goats and certified IBGA judges will always come to a meeting of the minds in the final placings."

"And, like, how do you get them to just stand there while the judge grabs their private parts?"

"Oh that's easy! You just reach over the goat and pick up its front leg on your opposite side. If the goat is too big for you, just reach down and pick up the front leg nearest you. This maneuver makes it difficult for the animal to charge through the audience with the judge jogging behind, holding the buck by his 'privates'. By the way, that reminds me. I was showing a buck at a show once, and the judge was checking those particular parts, and he looked up at the buck and said, "cough please." I just stared at him like he was crazy. When I came out of the ring my husband asked me what the judge said. When I told him, he laughed for two days, but he still won't explain the joke."

"Don't look at me, I'll ask my Veterinarian, OK? Annette, since you have been showing goats for over twenty years, what would you say is the most important thing about going to an IBGA show?"

"Well, I would like to say that it gets me away from the phone, but with pagers and cell phones that doesn't work anymore. The true answer is having the chance to visit with other Boer goat breeders. The opportunity to see how their breeding program is working. And above all, it is the best place to sell goats. The public comes to goat shows to see animals and have a chance to purchase stock. You can't sell goats if you stay in the barn!"

"Well, if I'm going to get out of the barn, I'd better get back to that big buck if I'm going to teach him anything. Talk to you later! Bye now!"♥

♥ This article was first printed in <u>The Goat Rancher Magazine</u> in July 1998.

Putting together a Flyer

Many people tell me that they could never send out flyers. They just would not know how to start. So I thought I would spend some time explaining a little about direct mail marketing.

First of all, you have to have a list of people to send it to. You can get lists of members to all of the registry associations,   including   the   American   Dairy   Goat Association, by calling them and ordering a list. Most of them will charge you a very nominal fee. There are addresses for all the registry associations, that I could find, in the Resources section of this book. These lists include the people that are actually interested in the breed of animal that you have to sell, or they are interested in goats in general. In addition, when someone calls you about goats, you should keep their phone number and address. Between all of these sources, you could mail to over 30,000 people.

Now, how do you make up a flyer? I always like to keep it short. It also needs to look good. I know that I am much *less* interested in reading a flyer that has been hand written, than one that is computer generated, and looks professional.   Most of us have been forced to buy a computer by now. It is time to find out how to use them. There are several programs that will help you to make professional looking flyers. These include Microsoft Word, Corel Draw, Microsoft Excel, and Quatro Pro. I have made flyers on all of these programs so I know it can be done. Sometimes you may have to look into some of the 'tool' or 'option' commands that you don't normally use, but it can be done. Once you have made the flyer, you can take it to any copy store and make as many copies as you want.

What do you put into the flyer? Well, if you are wanting to talk about meat goats, you might put together something like one of the examples on the next 2 pages, but please remember that they are only examples, and that I happen to raise Boer goats. When I start to write a flyer, I try to think of 5 points that I want people to know. Then I try to think of a format that won't immediately get thrown in the trash. I have played with different types of paper, different graphics, and different kinds of information. It is really up to you how you put it together.

WHY SHOULD YOU CONSIDER ADDING BOER MEAT GOATS TO YOUR RANCH?

* WHILE CATTLE PRICES CONTINUE TO FALL, MEAT GOAT PRICES ARE RISING DRAMATICALLY!

* THE BOER GOAT IS ONE OF THE HARDIEST OF ALL LIVESTOCK BREEDS.

* THE BOER GOAT HAS OUTSTANDING SIZE AND GROWTH RATE.

* BOER GOATS CAN ADD MEAT AND WEIGHT TO YOUR WEANING AGE DAIRY KIDS!

DON'T BE FOOLED! BUY ONLY SUPERIOR QUALITY BOER GOATS FROM BOWMAN BOER RANCH!

Flyer 1-inside

WE CARRY A LARGE SELECTION OF

* PUREBRED BOER BUCKS

* PUREBRED & 50% DOES BRED BACK TO BOER

* DOES WITH KIDS BY THEIR SIDE

CALL:
BOWMAN BOER RANCH

208-736-2575

BOWMAN BOER RANCH
P.O. BOX 1626
TWIN FALLS, ID 83303
208-736-2575

WHY

SHOULD YOU

RAISE

BOER MEAT

GOATS??

BBR

Flyer 1 – Outside of the trifold

Bowman Boer Ranch

'Premier Boer Goats for the Northwest'

DAVID

& GAIL

BOWMAN

'FABIO'
GRAND CHAMPION JUNIOR BUCK
REGION 1 IBGA SHOW

'FLAVIA'
GRAND CHAMPION JUNIOR DOE
REGION 1 IBGA SHOW

Our thanks to Hill Country Farms for selling us the embryos that won!

P.O. Box 1626 Twin Falls, ID 83303   208-736-2575   FAX 208-734-0832

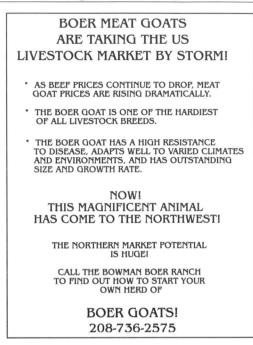

Experts give us the following advice about direct mailings:

> Know your audience.
> Don't assume your audience is stupid.
> Creative does not necessarily mean effective.
> If it doesn't work, try something different.
> Write as if you were talking to one person.
> Be complete and tell the truth.
> Good copy stresses reasons to purchase, serves a need, and backs up all claims with proof of value.
> Do not ramble.
> Do not use fear or negative inducements, stay positive.
> Stress the ease and convenience of your product.
> Appeal to the person's desire to be 'better', or 'more'.
> Write when you are relaxed, and in a pleasant environment.
> Urgency is vital. Always include a cutoff date or specific time limit for your offer.
> Always give a reason why I should take the action you want.
> Do not use slang.
> Don't be repetitive.

> Keep it simple.
> Long copy is OK if it is also all of the above points.
> Copy should be lean, concise and smooth flowing.[24]

Holding a Seminar or Management workshop

A great way to get serious breeders out to your ranch is to hold an event that they want to attend. Most registry associations would be happy to help you put on a seminar or field day, if they don't have to pick up the check. So, plan an event, and send out flyers, follow them up with phone calls, and get people to come over.

One type of event is a 'field day'. This is basically a goat management workshop where you set up mini-lectures and demonstrations on things like hoof trimming, showing goats, different feeds available in the area, registering your goats, etc. These events are usually associated with food. Barbecue some goat, buy some potato salad, and watch the people line up. However, these types of events usually cost money to put on. You can combine your event with the local dairy goat group, or the local 4-H group. You can charge, or ask for donations, for lunch. You can even charge a small entrance fee. If you have an event like this at your ranch, everyone will want to have a tour of your animals, and to know if you have anything for sale. If you don't want to give tours, have it somewhere else.

You can also hold a seminar by bringing in a guest speaker. This could be a judge, or an expert on a current issue. Again, food helps.

Put together a Web Page

The internet is becoming a very powerful sales tool. If you are not on the internet, you can skip this section. If you are on the internet, and you have goats to sell, you should start shopping around to people's web pages to see if you think you might want to do something similar. If you decide to look into the idea further, talk to some of the people whose web pages appeal to you. Most people have them made up by a professional, and I have found that people are amazingly excited to tell you who did it and how much it cost.

The people I have spoken with, who have web pages, have found them to be well worth the investment in sales. As we move forward, we may all have to learn to use the tools that work in our times.

Newspaper Articles

In many areas, the meat goat industry is still new enough to be news. Even in areas where it is old hack, there are new developments all the time. Think of something to tell the newspaper, like; "I am raising the animal that is on the leading edge of the small livestock industry.", or "I am using this great kind of animal to guard my livestock.", or "Goat meat is lower in fat than chicken.", or "I am having a seminar on my ranch". If they can come out and get pictures, they will often be very interested in a story. Especially if you live in a small town.

An article in the newspaper is free advertising. Many of us goat raisers are shy, but this is not as painful as you might think. A nice, interested, reporter just comes out and lets you ramble about your subject. Then they take some pictures, then they tell you when to check the papers. If they print your phone number, and they often do, you will have a bunch of calls the next day.

A word to the wise, though. Do not say anything that might get you in trouble later. Because they will print it, and it will come back to haunt you. So stay away from things like, "My neighbor's goats are smaller because they are all sick.", or "The (anything) company really doesn't do a very good job.", or "I can guarantee you that if you buy goats from me they will..."

Being Consistent

The hardest part of marketing is being consistent. We put so much of ourselves in every flyer, every article, and every event, that we just stop marketing for a while. To have consistent sales, you need to decide you are going to do something to market your animals on a regular basis. Then decide what that basis is for you. Whether it is yearly, quarterly, monthly, or whatever it is, you need to write it on your calendar and be consistent.

There is a pattern to all advertisers. We do a big advertising campaign; it works, so we feel great. Then we stop doing it because it worked. After a while, there are no more sales, and we say, "When did we last advertise?" As it turns out, it was over a year ago. Put it on your calendar and stick to your plan.

Contracts and Documentation

When you sell goats, it is a good idea to provide your buyers with whatever records you have about medical history, breeding records, registration papers, etc. That means you have to keep records. If you always vaccinate all the goats on your ranch in the month of January, you can write down for your buyer what you give them, and that you always do it in January. Even if your vaccination plan is more complicated, write it down. How hard can that be?

If you are selling registered stock you need to provide your buyers with the registration papers, certificates of transfer, bill of sale, and breeding records, with service memos, if they are pregnant.

If someone has promised to buy an animal, but has not put any money down, the animal is not sold. It is just too easy not to have the money when the time comes, and that is usually what happens. If you have taken a deposit on an animal, you need to have a contract, so all the people involved have the same understanding. I have been asked many times to publish my contracts. Well, here is a sample contract:

PURCHASE AND SALE AGREEMENT

DATE _____

YOUR RANCH agrees to sell and _____ agrees to buy the livestock listed below, in accordance with the following conditions:

ID#	NAME	BREED	TATOO	SEX	BD

CONDITIONS:

Further Conditions:

YOUR RANCH agrees that the above livestock may undergo a veterinary examination and be tested for any disease that the buyer requests, at the buyer's expense. This examination and testing may be arranged for by the buyer or by YOUR RANCH, to be done by any veterinarian of the buyer's choice. The examination and testing must be done on the premise of YOUR RANCH, and the livestock must not leave the premise of YOUR RANCH until the results of the testing have been received and accepted by both the buyer and YOUR RANCH.

The total purchase price is $____. A security deposit of $____ has been submitted to YOUR RANCH at the time of the signing of this agreement. The balance, $____, is due and payable at the time the livestock is picked up. We, the below signed, agree to the above described sale under the terms and conditions of this agreement.

_____   _____

We, the below signed, accept the above described livestock sale as final and agree that all conditions of this sale have been met to our satisfaction. We understand that the title and all risk of loss now passes to the buyer.

_____   _____

Please understand that I am not an attorney, and have no legal training. If you use this contract, and it fails in some way, I have not guaranteed it in any way. By the way, I have been told that I need to add a strong 'Hold Harmless' clause to all my contracts. You might want to look into that.

Conclusion

I hope I have given you some ideas about marketing your goats. I actually like to market. It gets to be fun. Be creative, and have a good time with it. Try new things. One of the best marketing campaigns my husband ever did for his business was having coffee cups made with a cute slogan on them, then passing them out to all his customers for Christmas. Years later people still had them sitting on their desks! Whatever your marketing plan, don't let frustration get to you if you don't immediately make sales. People keep flyers around for years, and pass them around to their neighbors. Sometimes it just takes a little while for marketing to produce fruit. Good luck!

NOTES:

10

Health Needs and Potential Problems

Health care is a vital issue for all ranchers. Disease has been described as "an absence of health", but when your animals are sick it seems more like the "plague of locusts". There is nothing more frustrating than standing by and watching your investment dwindle and die as your veterinarian bills sky-rocket!

Most health problems can be avoided by knowing the nutritional and housing needs of your animals, and consistently meeting those needs. If you have pregnant does that are due to kid within two months, you can usually avoid pregnancy toxemia by increasing the energy in your feed. If your animals are looking thin and have rough coats, check your worming schedule. Do you provide adequate and appropriate minerals for your feeding program? Do you vaccinate for diseases that are common in your area? Do you try to keep new animals away from the animals you have had longer to prevent introducing new problems to your herd? Do your animals have shelter from the weather? If you can answer "yes" to these basic questions, you are well on your way to a healthy herd.

Health management policies are as varied as the breeders who implement them. A large meat herd may do very little to diagnose and treat health problems, while a small breeding stock operation may do extensive blood testing as well as fecal exams for worms, and biannual vaccinations. The important thing to remember is that a healthy goat will grow faster and produce better than a sick goat. Many breeders, of all kinds of livestock, have discovered that you can usually make more money in increased production by worming and vaccinating your animals, and culling diseased animals, than you can save by doing little or nothing for them.

I am always frustrated by the misconceptions and misunderstandings that run rampant about specific potential health problems in a goat herd. For that reason, I am going to explain each issue as fully as I can, and then give you the resources to find out more about goat health care, if you want to. That does not mean that each and every issue is going to make or break your ranch, or even affect you at all. These are just things that you should understand. No one, with more than a few goats, can afford to test for every single possible problem that is out there. Don't make yourself crazy! YOU must decide, for YOUR operation, which issues are important enough that you need to deal with them.

Emergency Procedures and Possible Causes

"An ounce of prevention is worth a pound of cure" is certainly an adage to live by in the goat business! Anyone that raises livestock will eventually face some sort of emergency. However, most goat emergencies arise from an injury or a feed problem that might have been prevented if the breeder knew what to look for, and was paying attention when he saw it.

Now that I've said that, let me say this. Everyone has accidents. Anyone that has ever raised children knows that no matter what we do to try to "child proof" the house, that two year old will still find something to get in to. This is especially true on a large scale ranch, or on a ranch where the breeders (you) are not accustomed to, not only locking the gates behind your animals, but having to hide the key as well.   Goats are smart, inquisitive and mischievous.   The first year I raised goats I had innumerable escapes, one broken bone, two cases of bloat and several long gashes. Luckily, I learned to think ahead of the goats, and recognize and treat minor injuries myself.

Minor scrapes and cuts are pretty common around livestock. Most of the cuts on my ranch (both human and goat) used to come from barbed wire.   When we bought this ranch, it had miles of three strand barbed wire fences. We have since learned that it is going to take a lot more than three strands of barbed wire to keep the goats in, and have covered those fences with field fence. The goats used to love to slide under or over that barbed wire.   It was a game.   Even when it made long gashes in their backs, sides or stomachs.   Another common source of cuts and gashes are nails that have worked loose from fences and goat houses. Learn to carry around a hammer, and train your eye, and your hand, to pick up any screws, nails, pieces of wire or baling twine that happen to be laying around on the ground.

If you find a goat that has cut itself, here are some basic steps to follow. Check the extent of the bleeding. If the bleeding is minor, or has already stopped, the best thing you can do is clean the wound.   I have found that hydrogen peroxide is almost universally safe to use to clean wounds. We had a cat once that showed up with a terrible abscess on its leg. We took it to the veterinarian, who kept it for three days draining the wound and trying to get it to start healing. Finally, after a huge vet bill, I received back a cat with an even bigger problem than when it left! So I said, "It can't get any worse," and poured hydrogen peroxide in the wound.   Within a week the

*PLEASE NOTE: I am not a veterinarian and have no veterinary training. It is not my intention to give medical advice. Before you follow any suggestion printed in this book that might be construed as medical advice, or administer any drug or vaccine, ALWAYS seek the advice of a qualified veterinarian.

abscess was completely healed. Well, two years later, my husband had surgery on his leg. The doctor didn't realize that the incision was infected until it burst open on a Sunday afternoon. So what do you do? I closed my eyes and poured hydrogen peroxide in it to wash it out. When the doctor finally called, hours later, he said I had done just the right thing. Now, if it works for cats, and it was good enough for my husband, it is OK to use on goats!

If the severity of the cut is somewhere between a surface scrape to a pretty deep gash, but you don't think it needs stitching, clean it out with hydrogen peroxide, 1% iodine or Betadine. For deeper cuts, you should use a small, sterilized brush with your hydrogen peroxide to clean away any debris like grass, straw or manure. There are a wealth of antibiotic sprays available for this type of injury. Always have one on hand in the barn. Spray the wound with an antibiotic, then put a spray or ointment around the edges to keep the flies away. It will probably be healed in a couple days. Now go and check to make sure that goat's Tetanus shots are up to date! A Tetanus antitoxin shot could be a good preventive measure.

If the cut is more serious and there is a lot of bleeding, put a clean cloth over the wound and press hard to stop the bleeding. Don't keep taking your hand away to check on the bleeding! That defeats the purpose! If you find an exposed bleeding blood vessel, you may have to put a hemostat on it (another good thing to have in your vet kit). Don't put any sprays on it! Secure the bandage in place with either vet wrap or duct tape and head for the veterinarian. If your goat has lost a lot of blood, be sure to keep her warm with an old blanket until you can get her to the vet.

Puncture wounds are harder to deal with because you never know what is happening inside. If you have a puncture wound that you think might be deep, it is probably best to call the veterinarian.

Many times, a veterinarian will suggest a course of antibiotics after a serious injury. In any case, watch the animal for a couple of weeks to be sure the wound doesn't get infected, and the animal doesn't develop a fever, act depressed or go off her feed.

Bloat is a relatively common problem in goat herds. There are two kinds of bloat. Free gas bloat and frothy bloat. Either of these problems will make the left side of the flank bulge out drastically, and either of them can kill your goats.

In the case of free gas bloat, you can lightly "drum" on the bulging left side of the goat with your hand and hear a "ping" kind of sound, like a basketball when you thump on it. This kind of bloat occurs when the goat has eaten something that ferments rapidly (usually too much grain), is unable to burp gas off more quickly than it is formed, has something blocking the esophagus, or has one of several odd neurologic or muscular disorders of the esophagus. In other words, the circumstances are not normal. The goat has gotten into the grain or swallowed a piece of bailing twine or apple that won't go down, or has a genetic problem that constitutes culling.

If the animal is choking on a piece of apple, etc., they will be drooling because the saliva won't go down either. You must try to clear the esophagus by reaching in and pulling out the obstruction. If they are bloating because of one of the other problems described above, you can carefully pass a long tube (it has to be long enough to reach their rumen) down the left side of the animal's throat and into the rumen. If the goat seems to be fighting for air, or you can feel them breathing through the tube, or the tube won't go down very far, you missed. A goat can easily bite through the tube, causing more problems, so be sure to put something hard into their mouth next to the tube for them to bite on (Besides your finger. A roll of white medical tape works well.). This is a bit of a trick to do, and a dying goat is no one's favorite guinea pig, but most of us refuse to learn these things until we need them.

Once the tube is past the esophagus, (You should be able to feel it pass through the esophagus if you put your fingers on the goat's neck.) put enough in to reach all the way to the rumen. Then, put the other end into a bucket of clean water. You will be able to see bubbles in the water, and smell an awful smell as gas is released. To get the gas to leave, you may actually have to have your helper push on the rumen with their hands. Do this slowly! A goat that has bloated badly has a circulation problem in all that super tight skin. Releasing the gas too fast can cause a heart attack. Push a few seconds, then let her rest a minute, then push a few seconds.

Frothy bloat sometimes occurs when ruminants eat lush legumes such as alfalfa or clover, and/or are on a ration consisting of a lot of finely ground concentrates. Molasses blocks treated with a bloat inhibitor are highly recommended if your animals are on rich legume pasture. To treat frothy bloat you cannot use a stomach tube. Give the goat poloxalene, oil of turpentine or (my favorite) liquid dish soap. These agents will reduce the surface tension of the tiny bubbles causing the goat to burp them out, or causing them to form one huge bubble, which will allow you to use a stomach tube.

What are the preventative measures for bloat? Pick up string and baling twine! Keep the grain in goat-proof containers (a little like child proof lids) that they really can't figure out how to open. Keep the goats away from the area the grain is stored (in the goat-proof containers). Don't change diets suddenly, and be sure your pasture has a good measure of non-legume grass in it. Don't feed chunks of apple or carrot to your goats unless they are cut up very small. Feed bloat inhibiting blocks when in doubt. You can even pre-treat your high legume pasture with one of various products manufactured to reduce the risk of bloat.

Anaphylactic shock is a devastating way to lose an animal. They say the best preventative is to have epinephrine at your side every time you give an injection. Many drugs that we routinely give our goats can cause anaphylactic shock, including C & D Perfringens, tetanus antitoxin and penicillin.   Symptoms include trembling, collapse, difficulty breathing, distress and/or bleating, hives, seizures and death.   The animal can die within minutes. There is no time to get a vet. Always watch your animals for 15 to 20 minutes after any kind of injection. Also, always pull back on the syringe before giving an injection to be sure you aren't in a vein!

Last year I was giving baby shots to some newborns (something that is difficult for me to do anyway).   I gave a pair of twins their shots and moved on to the next set. The first set just kept crying even after I gave them back to their mother.   My helpers told me I was being silly to worry, so I went ahead and gave the shots to the third set. The first set was still crying.   So I went to look.   Their little faces were so swollen up that they could hardly see!   Well, I scooped them up and ran into the house to called the vet.   The answering service said he would call me back later.   Later!   I didn't know what to do!   The only thing I could think of was some liquid antihistamine I bought for my nephew who had asthma.   So I gave them some of that. I have no idea how much I gave them, but it worked. Within minutes the swelling had gone down and they wanted Mama again.   The veterinarian called me the next day. I went out and bought some epinephrine.

Fractured bones will sometimes occur, even on a truly well managed ranch.   The best thing to do is restrain the animal and take it to the veterinarian.   Splints can sometimes be applied, but they can be harmful if used incorrectly.   Some, very tough, goat ranchers actually cast their animal's breaks themselves, but I tend to think there must be some reason those veterinarians spend all that time at school.   How to set a bone, and avoid shock and infection as a result, must surely be one of those reasons!

How do you prevent breaks?   Look around and think. When we first started, we brought in all kinds of "toys" for our baby goats to frolic on. Some of these were assorted large wooden wire spools. They were supposed to jump off of them and play "king of the mountain". Which they certainly did. However, it probably took the kids a week to figure out that it was fun to stick their hooves into the holes in thc top of those spools, and then watch while that hoof miraculously reappeared when they pulled it back out! Great fun! Until someone else wanted to be "king of the mountain" while that hoof was still in the hole. "Ouch!" We don't give the kids spools to play with anymore.

Poisonings due to something other than poisonous plants (poisonous plants are discussed in the chapter entitled "Feeding for Production") can happen occasionally. If you suspect you may have old paint on your ranch that contains lead, you should take a sample to your county health department and get it tested. Lead poisoning is rare in these days of environmentally safe paint, but it can still happen. Arsenic and urea are two chemicals that are pretty common in the barn/gardening shed and should be carefully locked away from goats.

Copper poisoning can occur through the ingestion of copper-containing footbath solution, or even horse feed with a high copper content. Goats are not as susceptible to copper poisoning in standard feeds as sheep are, and can even become copper deficient if restrained from all sources of copper in an attempt to keep them from being poisoned.

Nitrates and organic phosphates in fertilizers can poison your goats if they are allowed to graze a newly fertilized pasture or get into the fertilizer sack in the barn. Some seed can be treated with pesticides, although goats would be just as likely to die from suddenly ingesting large amounts of the seed, as from the pesticide. When you use herbicides and pesticides on your pastures be sure to follow label directions and keep your goats off the pasture at least as long as the manufacturer suggests!

If you think your goats might be poisoned, try to discover the source, then call your veterinarian for advice. There are different treatments for different poisons.

Normal Goat Statistics:
Body Temperature: 102.5 to 104 degrees F
(body temperature can vary due to outside air temperature and activity)
Pulse/heart rate: 60 to 80 beats per minute
Respiration rate: 15 to 30 breaths per minute
Puberty: 4 to 12 months
Estrus ("heat") cycle: 18 to 23 days
Length of "heat":   12 to 36 hours
Gestation: 145 to 155 days

Worms, Parasites and Fungi

Stomach and intestinal worms can have extremely harmful effects in goats when present in large numbers. The control of internal parasites is dependent upon a management program which will minimize the ingestion of worm larvae along with a medication program designed to kill a maximum number of worms in the goat. For information about the type of worms that are the most prevalent in your area, and the best wormers to combat them, it is a good idea to talk to your county extension agent and a good veterinarian. Many vets will suggest that you bring in fecal samples to be checked so you can better understand the worms in your specific herd. It is also a good idea to rotate the type of wormer you use.

Liver flukes are prevalent in areas where slugs and snails are common, because they require snails as a carrier. Most often, you will find these pests to be a problem in marshy lowlands, but they are also very common on

*PLEASE NOTE: I am not a veterinarian and have no veterinary training. It is not my intention to give medical advice. Before you follow any suggestion printed in this book that might be construed as medical advice, or administer any drug or vaccine, ALWAYS seek the advice of a qualified veterinarian.

irrigated pastures. Symptoms include marked depression, abdominal pain, chronic weight loss, anemia, weakness, facial edema, and sudden death. Diagnosis may require laboratory assistance so it is definitely the job for a veterinarian.[25]

Lungworms can cause severe verminous pneumonia in goats and are also prevalent in areas where slugs and snails are common, because they require snails as a carrier. Lungworms are most likely to occur in cool, wet autumnal weather when younger stock, on lowlands or irrigated pastures, ingest (eat) larvae or snails. The worms produce eggs which are coughed onto the ground. The eggs are then re-swallowed by another goat, and hatch during intestinal passage. Diagnosis is very difficult and will require the help of your veterinarian.[25]

Nematodes are stomach worms. They include such common names as round worms, Barber's pole worms and wire worm. The larvae are ingested (eaten) when your goats eat forage or feed that has been inoculated with fecal pellets containing the larvae. Warm, moist soil surface conditions favor propagation of the worms, while hot dry or extremely cold conditions are detrimental to the larvae survival. This is a great reason not to feed on the ground!

Signs of infection include acute anemia, facial edema (Bottle Jaw), weak and listless behavior, and ultimately death. Diarrhea frequently occurs with heavy infestation. Young animals and females 30 days before or after kidding are the most vulnerable.

This is how the worms get into your goats: The goat eats the grass or feed that contains nematode larvae. The larvae are then transmitted to the stomach where they develop into adults. The females release the eggs, which are then transmitted to the ground via fecal pellets. Once on the ground, the eggs hatch producing more larvae and the whole process starts over again. Some nematodes can over-winter in the host in a dormant state. The best defense against nematodes is to rotate your pasture and worm your goats.[26]

Wormers available to U.S. sheep and goat producers

Class of Compound		Effective against:			
Active Ingredient	Trade Name:	Nema -tode	Tape- worm	Lung- worm	Liver- fluke
Avermectin					
Ivermectin	Ivomec	*		*	* I-Plus
Benzimidazoles					
Albendazole	Valbazen	*	*	*	*
	Safe-Guard	*	*	*	
	Panacur	*	*	*	
	Telmin	*			
	Synanthic	*	*	*	
	Benzelmin	*	*	*	
	Anthelcide	*			
Imidothiazole					
Levamisole	Tramisole	*	*	*	
	Levasol	*	*	*	

Chart 1:** Wormers available to U.S. sheep and goat producers: Any reference to commercial products or trade names is made with the understanding that this chart is for educational purposes and no discrimination or endorsement is intended. [26]

** Not all of these products are approved for use in goats, so it is always a good idea to check with your veterinarian before using any drug. Many drugs are not a good idea during pregnancy or lactation (wormers are poisons) and you should always double check drug withdrawal times before butchering. Many kinds of worms can become resistant to a wormer if it is used over long periods of time. It is always a good idea to rotate your wormers annually or biannually. When rotating, you should switch to a product from a different family. For instance, don't switch from aldendazole to fenbendazole because they are both in the Benzimidazole family.

*PLEASE NOTE: I am not a veterinarian and have no veterinary training. It is not my intention to give medical advice. Before you follow any suggestion printed in this book that might be construed as medical advice, or administer any drug or vaccine, ALWAYS seek the advice of a qualified veterinarian.

Tapeworms, when present in large numbers, can cause emaciation. Tapeworms are prevalent in the geographic areas where slugs and snails are common. Not all wormers are effective against tapeworms, so read your labels carefully. A very heavy tapeworm infestation is a good reason to consult with a veterinarian. They can be very hard to kill!

Ringworm and related fungi are common in goats, and appear as circles or patches of whitish crusty skin where the hair has fallen out. Fungi prefer moist dark areas and really hate sunshine, so one treatment is for spring to finally show up after a long winter! Treatment includes iodine washes, fungicidal sprays, iodine sprays, and my vet recommends a small amount of Captan@ (*note: Captan is a carcinogen. If you use it, be careful not to get it on you.*) dissolved in water and then used as a wash. If the goat has a bad case, you will gain better results from your treatment if you shave the hair away from the infected area first.

Sore Mouth (Contagious Ecthyma) is very common in goats, and usually infects nursing kids. Papules and vesicles followed by scabs develop most commonly on the lips, eyelids, teats, and scrotum and persist for 3 to 4 weeks. The infection spreads primarily through contact with the sores. However, dried scabs that have fallen to the ground may remain infective for years so that once the disease appears on the ranch, you can expect to see it every year.[43] Mastitis or starvation of the kids may occur when the lesions involve the teats. An ointment should be applied to keep the teats pliable. Many ranchers assure me that iodine helps to keep the sores from getting infected. This virus is so insidious that kids can give it to their mothers by nursing, and many people say that once it is on your ranch, all your kids will get it. Generally, the disease must run its course and treatment should only be considered if secondary bacterial infection occurs. Be sure to wear gloves when handling sore mouth as it is transmittable to humans! There is a vaccine, but ranchers that have never had the infection on their ranch are often reluctant to use it, because once you vaccinate, you will have to continue vaccinating every year or you will have the disease from the scabs caused by the vaccine.[25]

Picture 31: Doe with sore mouth.[*]

Other Parasites and Infections

Abscesses, Cellulitis and Foreign Bodies.   Goats are very susceptible to various lumps and bumps.   Any splinter or cut is likely to develop into an infection causing a lump.   In most cases, the appropriate treatment is to lance the lump and carefully clean it out with hydrogen peroxide.   Many veterinarians recommend packing the clean incision with a small amount of penicillin.   If there is a splinter or other foreign body, be sure you get it out.

- This picture donated by Emma's Dream Farm from Ellensburg, Washington.

*PLEASE NOTE: I am not a veterinarian and have no veterinary training. It is not my intention to give medical advice. Before you follow any suggestion printed in this book that might be construed as medical advice, or administer any drug or vaccine, ALWAYS seek the advice of a qualified veterinarian.

Many times a vaccination may leave a lump that fills with white blood cells then will either just go away or burst in time. None of these conditions are a problem unless Caseous Lymphadenitis bacteria (Corynebacterium pseudotuberculosis) has been introduced into the system (see Caseous Lymphadenitis later in this chapter). If you see a lump and your goat is running a fever, losing weight, moping around or off her feed, call your veterinarian immediately.[27]

Coccidiosis is caused by protozoal parasites that are resistant and non-responsive to de-wormers. They are present in the small intestines of all animals and become a problem due to contamination of feed and water. This is often a problem with young kids that are raised on a bottle because of the need to have them in a relatively confined, warm area. The symptoms are bloody diarrhea (black and sticky), dehydration and death. However, sometimes the kids can die before diarrhea starts. Ranchers should know that this disease can be spread by birds, so those people that have chickens, turkeys, pigeons, etc., should be extra careful. Coccidiosis can be prevented with Decoquinate and treated with sulfa drugs and amprolium. I use a commonly available sulfa drug for livestock, every day, in very small doses, right in the milk for my bottle fed kids, to both treat and prevent Coccidiosis (follow label directions carefully).[28]

Foot Rot infection may be introduced to the herd by an infected sheep or goat and it is hardest to eradicate on ranches where sheep are also present. Foot rot flourishes in warm, moist environments. Lameness, sole separation and a foul odor are typical symptoms. Treatment includes radical trimming of the hoof and medicated foot baths. Udder irritation may occur when using a foot bath unless an absorbent material such as peat moss is placed in the foot bath to prevent splashing.[29]

Lice and Mange causing mites are common in goats. Usually, these pests do not pose a threat to healthy animals housed in conditions where they can get plenty of fresh air and sunshine. Many of us however, find the little things unacceptable as they cause itching and blood loss even in healthy goats. There are several products that are very good for pest control on goats. These include a wide range of pour-ons, powders and injectables. When treating for lice or mites the entire herd must be treated the same day.

Screw worms, Ticks and Flies are an ever present nuisance with any livestock. Any sign of an open wound or blood should be promptly sprayed with a screw worm insecticide available at your local feed store or animal supply store (ointments are also available). Again, there are plenty of pour-on type products that will control ticks and flies on your animals. As far as flies in your barns or pastures, my best recommendation is always cleanliness. If your barn is clean and there isn't a buildup of manure in your pens, you won't have as many flies. The animal supply stores now have handy little machines that put a measured burst of insecticide into the air every 10 to 15 minutes. These neat little wonders are approved for food preparation sites and dairies. I have them in each of my goat houses and barns for the most effective control of flies that I have ever seen. You can also buy parasitic wasps that feed on fly larva. They use these in the South, and I have heard they work very well.

Diseases

Brucellosis or Bang's Disease (Brucella melitensis) is extremely rare in the United States (even the few cases reported in the U.S. in recent memory appear to be very questionable). Any animals coming into the U.S. from other countries are required to be vaccinated (as are cattle in the U.S.). Brucellosis causes abortion in the last trimester of pregnancy, pneumonia, encephalitis,

PLEASE NOTE: I am not a veterinarian and have no veterinary training. It is not my intention to give medical advice. Before you follow any suggestion printed in this book that might be construed as medical advice, or administer any drug or vaccine, ALWAYS seek the advice of a qualified veterinarian.

meningitis and spondylitis in goats. The organism is shed in the urine, milk, and vaginal discharges. Brucellosis is highly infectious to humans causing Malta fever. Any suspected case must be reported to state and federal veterinary services. There are laboratory tests available for this disease. *If your goats are suspected of having Brucellosis, I would strongly question that diagnosis and be sure the tests are sent to a federally approved laboratory for conformation!* [30] [31]

CAE or CAEV (Caprine arthritis-encephalitis virus) is a common disease of goats that is prevalent worldwide. In the United States, prevalence as high as 81% has been reported for goat herds. According to a recent study by J. D. Rowe, DVM, "Infection most commonly occurs when the virus is present in colostrum or milk that is ingested. However, prolonged contact, particularly in high-density goat populations, also results in significant transmission." [32] Not all CAEV infections in kids can be explained by ingestion of affected colostrum or milk. Up to 10% of kids from positive dams, who were removed from their mothers at birth, have been reported to show infection. In these cases, infection must have occurred in one of four ways: 1. in-utero transmission, 2. transmission from the dam by vaginal contact, 3. accidental ingestion of infected colostrum, 4. transmission from the dam by exposure to saliva or respiratory secretions during licking.

CAEV infection may not be serologically testable for months or years, and some infected animals, who can transmit the disease, may never show clinical symptoms. Symptoms include a progressive rear leg weakness and/or paralysis in kids 2 to 6 months of age, chronic arthritis (most frequently, but not solely, of the knee joint) in adults, inflammation of the mammary gland, lung, and nervous system. Nervous system involvement may include blindness, head tilts, and facial nerve paresis. Mammary involvement results in "udder edema" or "hard udder" where the entire udder becomes hard and warm within the first few hours after kidding, resulting in the kids going hungry. [33] (This is not to be confused with the doe that has so much milk at kidding that she needs to be

milked in addition to nursing her kids.) Lung involvement
results in chronic pneumonia.

In a milking herd, shared milking machines, milk
contaminated hands or towels, etc. will significantly
increase the risk of spreading the disease. In a meat herd,
transmission can occur via needles, tattooing instruments
or dehorning equipment. Also cited by P. L. Greenwood as
possible avenues of infection, in high density herds that
are endemically infected, are head butting to the point of
drawing blood, eye-licking, biting, snorting and coughing,
and urinating too near another goat's face.[34] In addition,
according to Rowe and East, sexual contact has been
researched with some definite indications that the risk of
infection in the exchange of saliva, estrus mucus, urine,
semen and nasal secretions, is possible. [32]

The period of time between exposure to CAEV and
development of detectable (testable) antibody levels has
been estimated, by researchers, at between 3 weeks to 8
months after exposure to the disease.[35] [36] [37]   Many
ranches have reported conversion from negative test
results to positive test results of goats as old as five years
of age, although conversion seems to be most prevalent
between 1 and 2 years of age.   Researchers attribute
conversions later than two years of age to some lateral
exposure to the disease as discussed in the last
paragraph.

The following steps are recommended to prevent CAEV
transmission: 1. Immediately remove the kids from their
dams at birth, if the dam is suspect (with the sack intact
until the kid is out of its mother's body, if possible), being
careful to prevent the does from licking their kids. Then
take the kid inside and wash it in warm water, in a clean
sink. 2. Provide heat treated, artificial or cow colostrum.
Do not pool colostrum from mothers that might be
infected and then feed the pooled colostrum to your
isolated kids!   3. Feed pasteurized or powdered milk.

*PLEASE NOTE: I am not a veterinarian and have no veterinary
training. It is not my intention to give medical advice. Before you follow
any suggestion printed in this book that might be construed as medical
advice, or administer any drug or vaccine, ALWAYS seek the advice of a
qualified veterinarian.*

4. Separate all possibly infected animals from uninfected animals by a double fence with at least 10 feet between the fences. Do not use common feeders, waterers or salt blocks. 5. Milk negative and younger does before milking positive and older does. 6. When possible, breed negative does with negative bucks. If negative and positive animals are mated, use a single hand-mating allowing minimal oral contact. 7. Do not share needles, tattooing equipment or dehorning devices without careful cleaning and sterilization. 8. Test (and cull) your goats at 6 month intervals starting after the kids are at least 4 months old. Most breeders suggest testing during times of stress, such as about 2 to 3 weeks before kidding. *There is, however, some evidence to suggest that a goat with <u>another type of systemic infection</u> may test with a false positive for CAEV.*[32]♥

Caseous Lymphadenitis is a chronic bacterial infection that causes external and internal lumps in sheep and goats. It is caused by a bacteria, Corynebacterium Pseudotuberculosis, which enters the body through a wound in the skin causing an infection and a slow growing, firm abscess. This infection may also travel to the regional lymph nodes causing a localized abscess there.

The disease is infectious and, under certain circumstances, can spread quickly through your herd. Not all abscesses are caused by this bacteria! In fact, relatively few abscesses are actually C.L. In order for the disease to be present, you must first have the bacteria in your herd or on your ranch. This usually occurs when an infected animal is brought into the herd. Secondly, there must be an entrance wound for the animal to get the bacteria into their systems. It is not necessarily true that an animal with no abscesses will not be carrying the bacteria, because the lesions can be on any part of the body including the internal organs. Usually the disease is

---

♥ This article on CAEV was first released as part of a article entitled "CAE What does it Mean to You?" in the "Goat Magazine", 4-98.

diagnosed when several animals in the herd are noticed to have a lump or string of lumps in the area of the lymph nodes. Abscesses can be removed or carefully cleaned out and, if there is no lymph node involvement, may not return. A sample of the pus in the abscess or of the animal's blood can be sent to one of the laboratories, which specialize in diagnosing this type of disease, for analysis. Pus from draining abscesses contains very large numbers of bacteria and the organism can survive for long periods (months) in the environment. This disease is transmittable (although cases are rare) to humans! So if you suspect C.L., let your veterinarian be the one to handle the abscess.

Recommended treatments and prevention programs are: 1. Don't introduce infected animals to your herd. 2. Cull affected goats. 3. Treat any affected goats that you cannot cull by promptly having the abscess cleaned out or removed. 4. Remove any sources of possible nicks and scrapes in your pastures and goat houses. 5. Vaccines are available in Australia and South Africa, and will hopefully be available to us here in the West in the near future. [27] [38]

Chlamydia psittaci is by far the most common cause of infectious abortion in goats. Chlamydia is a viral disease that is thought to be transmitted by ingestion. Newborn females may also acquire the infection at birth, carrying it through to their first pregnancy. Abortion usually occurs in the last four weeks of gestation, but can occur as early as the 100th day of gestation. Does are not normally ill but some may develop retained placenta following abortion. However, once a doe has aborted, she is immune and the immunity will usually last at least three years. Therefore, a herd with an endemic Chlamydia infection will have abortions only in young does and new additions to the herd. Laboratory tests have been

---

*PLEASE NOTE: I am not a veterinarian and have no veterinary training. It is not my intention to give medical advice. Before you follow any suggestion printed in this book that might be construed as medical advice, or administer any drug or vaccine, ALWAYS seek the advice of a qualified veterinarian.

developed for this disease, however animals that have been vaccinated may test positive. [30]

Enterotoxemia due to Clostridium perfringens type C and D is very common in goats. This disease occurs primarily in young, rapidly growing animals usually resulting in sudden death. As a preventative measure, does should receive a C & D perfringens toxoid injection late in their pregnancy, and kids should receive an injection of C & D perfringens antitoxin at birth, and then C & D perfringens toxoid vaccinations at 3 or 4 weeks of age and then again as recommended on the package. Some sources feel that vaccinations should be twice annually rather than once a year, or even as much as every 60 days if your goats are confined and fed a grain ration daily, for effective control of the disease. An important part of prevention is the control of feed intake in order to limit the amount of undigested starches in the small intestine. Any changes in feed programs should always be done slowly. Particular attention should be given to intakes of grain, bakery goods, fresh green feeds to goats who are unaccustomed to green feed, and to milk intake in very young animals. [20] [21 43 39]

The aluminum phosphate adjuvant in the available C & D perfringens vaccines can result in raised skin lesions in goats. Most of these reactions regress within 6 months but a few may persist and subsequently rupture. These should not be a cause for concern, but should a lesion rupture, the area should be cleaned and treated with a good preparation to keep the flies away.[40]

Iodine Deficiency (Congenital) in newborn animals is characterized by thick scaly skin, an enlarged thyroid gland (or goiter) and general weakness. The herd usually has a history of low reproductive efficiency and a high incidence of abortions and neonatal deaths. Iodine deficiency usually results from an inadequate intake of iodine in the feed and water, although it can also occur with the excessive consumption of some plants. The inclusion of iodized salt in the mineral ration will usually prevent this condition.[41]

Johne's Disease (Paratuberculosis) is one of the diseases that cause chronic weight loss in adult goats. This disease is caused by a bacteria called Mycobacterium Paratuberculosis. This organism is shed in the feces of infected adults and can stay in the environment for many months. New infections occur in newborn or young animals that are exposed to a contaminated environment. The bacteria are ingested (eaten), then localize in the gastrointestinal tract and adjacent lymph nodes and stay in a dormant state for long periods. Clinical signs are almost never seen before 1 year of age, and include progressive weight loss, which may continue for weeks or months. Appetite usually remains good, but the animal becomes increasingly lethargic and depressed. Goats rarely show the diarrhea that is typical of cattle with this disease. This disease can be positively diagnosed with laboratory testing. [25] [42]

Listeriosis is a caused by the bacteria Listeria monocytogenes. The development and sporadic occurrence of this disease is very poorly understood. Outbreaks often occur about three weeks after a herd is started on corn silage. However, the disease also occurs in herds that have never been fed corn silage. The bacteria are carried by many types of wildlife and birds, and can survive in the soil for years in spite of freezing temperatures. One form of this disease causes encephalitis or brain inflammation. Symptoms include fever, confusion, circling, and facial paralysis on one side with drooping of the one ear, eyelid and lip. This disease is very acute in goats, usually causing death in 24 hours

Listeriosis can also cause septicemia or abortion. Be very careful when handling aborted fetuses or sick animals, and do not drink the milk of infected goats, because this disease can infect humans! Treatments involve high dosages of antibiotics. However, the goat is usually dead before the drugs can take affect. Prevention is difficult

*PLEASE NOTE: I am not a veterinarian and have no veterinary training. It is not my intention to give medical advice. Before you follow any suggestion printed in this book that might be construed as medical advice, or administer any drug or vaccine, ALWAYS seek the advice of a qualified veterinarian.

since the organism is widespread and its mode of infection is unclear. The best present recommendation is to introduce silage very slowly into the diet, and to avoid spoiled silage entirely.[43] [44]

Mastitis is the inflammation of the mammary gland. The milk from udders with mastitis is usually discolored and is clotted or stringy. The udder itself will be warm, swollen or lumpy looking and painful. Do not use or feed the milk of a doe that has mastitis! If a doe freshens with mastitis, the kids can die from starvation before you realize what is wrong. It never hurts to go out and check the milk flow from a new mother's teats at least twice in the first few days after kidding, even if you have a large meat herd. If you suspect your doe has mastitis, check with your veterinarian as soon as possible. Mastitis can usually be avoided by using good sanitary procedures and a teat dip while hand or machine milking, and by drying off the doe properly when she has finished nursing or being milked. [33]

Polioencephalomalacia is caused by either a thiamine deficiency or an inhibition of thiamine activity. Dietary and management factors that may alter normal rumen flora appear to play a key role in the development of this disease. Sudden changes in feed, the feeding of moldy hay, the dietary stress of weaning, and overdosing of amprolium wormers, have all been associated with cases of polioencephalitis. Early signs may include depression, anorexia and/or diarrhea with gradual occurrence of neurologic abnormalities over 1 to 7 days. These abnormalities include excitability, elevation of the head while standing, staring off into space, circling, muscle tremors and apparent blindness.

The only effective treatment is thiamine injections. If the disease is caught early enough, complete recovery can be expected. B complex vitamins contain thiamine, and can be used if thiamine is not available. If you suspect this disease, involve your veterinarian immediately. If the veterinarian is not available, you can try giving the goat a vitamin B complex injection in the muscle. Then find your vet. Only very prompt treatment will save your goat.[39]

Pregnancy Toxemia (Ketosis) occurs during the last 2 to 6 weeks of gestation in does that have experienced a reduction of feed intake, are in poor condition, are having more than two kids (or very large kids), or are very fat. This makes more sense when you consider that eighty percent of the fetal growth occurs in the last six weeks of pregnancy, and does that are out of condition, or whose fat or sheer fetal mass get in the way of their rumen capacity, will have trouble taking in enough nutrition to meet the drastically increased nutritional needs of the fetus. In does that produce a lot of milk, ketosis can also occur during early lactation. This disease results from a negative ratio of energy utilized compared with energy taken in. Does may go off by themselves, have a poor appetite, run into objects and appear blind, have swelling of the lower limbs, stand with their noses pointed to ward the sky, or stand with their heads pressed against a wall or fence for hours. As the disease progresses, muscle twitching, circling and spasmodic twitching of the head may occur. Accurate diagnosis can be facilitated by using a diabetic ketone test strip for the urine. If untreated, death can occur within three or four days.

Ketosis is preventable by feeding does a lowered grain ration, or none at all if your feed and/or pasture is good, during periods when they are not milking, and also at the beginning of their pregnancy, to keep them from getting too fat. Then increasing the grain (energy) ration gradually during the last two months of pregnancy and maintaining it at a reasonable level (between one and two pounds per day per doe) through early lactation. If you think your doe may have Ketosis you should consult your veterinarian. Treatment includes the administration of 20 to 60 ccs of propylene glycol, two or three times a day. Propylene glycol is available from most feed stores. A little molasses or Karo syrup in some warm water might help her to hold on until the vet can arrive. This mix is also a good idea for a treat after kidding (I have heard of ranchers who use Gatoraide® after kidding, too). [30] [43]

Q Fever (Coxiella burnetii) is widespread in livestock. Q Fever causes abortion in the last 2 to 4 weeks of pregnancy. This disease is shed through the milk as well as through the fetus, placenta and uterine tissues. Humans can be infected causing flu-like symptoms. For this reason, any aborted fetuses should always be disposed of very carefully. [30]

Scrapie is a disease of sheep that is starting to receive some attention from the goat industry because of the increased number of animals coming into the United States and Canada for the meat goat industry. Scrapie is a progressive, fatal nervous disease of mature animals. The disease is characterized by an altered gait, tremors of the head and neck, incessant rubbing against inanimate objects, skin biting and progressive weight loss in spite of a normal appetite. At this time, very little information on Scrapie testing is available. If you would like to test your animals, or you suspect your goats may have this disease, contact your veterinarian for help.[44]

Tetanus or "Lockjaw" is a common threat in any animal herd. This wound infection disease most often occurs with deep penetrating wounds, castration and elastrator banding. The interval between infection and clinical signs may range from four days to several weeks. The main symptom is muscle stiffness particularly in the legs, muscles of the jaw, and around the wound itself. Stiffness progresses rapidly and muscle rigidity increases. The animal will stiffen into a 'saw horse' position, have difficulty chewing or swallowing, and movement becomes impossible. Death is a respite. Prevention includes the injection of Tetanus antitoxin at birth followed by Tetanus toxoid shots at three to four weeks old, and then annually. (Some recent studies suggest that Tetanus antitoxin may cause a large number of the anaphylactic shock reactions in goats, so use care with this drug.) Sterilization of any surgical equipment and careful attention to cleanliness around wounds is important. Any deep wound warrants a Tetanus antitoxin shot along with normal treatment.[43]

Toxoplasmosis is caused by the protozoan Toxoplasma gondii and is a cause of abortion, mummification, stillbirth and birth of weak kids in goats. Cats become carriers by eating infected placentas or rodents, then shed the disease in their feces. This disease is a very good reason to cover your pellet and grain storage bins to keep the cats from using them as litter boxes.[39]

Urinary Calculi (Urolithiasis) is fairly common in bucks and should be understood by everyone who has put the majority of their investment into their herd sire. This disease is characterized by the formation of calculi within the urinary tract blocking or partially blocking the urethra. This causes retention of urine, abdominal pain, distention and rupture of the urethra or bladder, and death. Urolithiasis is caused by a nutritional imbalance and is a problem in bucks (but seldom in does) because of the structure of their urinary tract. It can happen at any age, although the animals at highest risk are castrated males, because the urinary tract stops growing and maturing when the animal is castrated. Symptoms include abdominal discomfort with colic, signs of restlessness, straining, kicking at the belly, and frequent attempts to urinate, as well as rapid twitching of the tail. The buck will isolate himself, refuse to eat and drink, act distressed, and then die. The total course of the disease is only 5 to 7 days!

Prevention of this disease is extremely important to all goat raisers and requires at least a basic understanding of the nutritional components of the feed or pasture you are using. The most common calculi problems are associated with grain rations high in dietary phosphorus. You should provide a 1.5 to 1 calcium to phosphorus (calcium 1.5 times as high as phosphorus) in the total feed ration. Feeding free choice minerals that are too high in phosphorus is a very bad idea. Common salt should be added to the diet of your bucks (free choice or in block form). Salt has an ionic action that seems to help calculi to pass through the system. The addition of vitamin A to the diet may also be helpful. Additional protection may be obtained through the use of ration additives such as ammonium chloride or potassium chloride which will acidify the urine.[45] Always have a ready supply of clean, warm water available. If you suspect that your buck is having trouble urinating, call your veterinarian immediately.[46]

Vesicular Stomatitis is a viral disease that is thought to be transmitted by insects as well as by direct contact with the fluids from infected animals' blisters (vesicles). The first sign of the disease is excessive salivation, followed by a fever and the appearance of blisters or whitened and raised vesicles in and around the mouth, nose, hooves and teats. These blisters swell and break, leaving raw, painful sores. Infected animals typically lose weight, because they are unable to eat or drink adequately. The incubation period is two to eight days after exposure, and the disease runs its course in two to three weeks. Risk of death is from secondary infection or starvation, not from the disease. Animal health officials are requiring veterinarians to report suspected cases in some states, and many states are requiring tests before animals are moved. Blood tests are available for this disease. Extreme caution should be practiced when handling infected animals because this disease is transmittable to humans.[47] [48] [43]

White Muscle Disease, or Selenium-vitamin E Deficiency, is very prevalent in kids from birth to several weeks old. The kid's muscles become sore and feel firm and he may be unable to rise, but their appetite is good and they will nurse readily if held. Older kids and adults may occasionally show signs of stiffness and a straddling gait especially after sever stress or vigorous exercise. *If you live in a selenium deficient area*, prevention includes providing selenium in the mineral ration, injecting does with selenium and vitamin E one month before kidding, and/or injecting the kids at birth and possibly again at 3 to 4 weeks of age.[49]

Hoof Trimming

Hoof Trimming is an acquired skill that takes quite a bit of practice to perfect. The tools you will need include a good pair of hoof shears. Do not try to save money on this particular tool. My favorite is called a "sheep foot rot shear". Hoof trimming shears are available in any animal supply house and come in many shapes and designs. You will also need a hand held carpenter's plane, the kind that looks a little like a cheese grater.

Hooves that are overgrown will turn under around the sides and may even grow out in front like elf shoes.

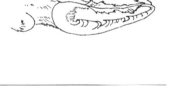

Start by cleaning the manure and crud out from the toes with a hoof pick or the point of your shears. Then trim off the overgrown sides down to the white sole.

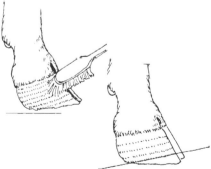

Now take a tooth brush and some water and scrub the sides of the hoof until you can see the little growth lines that are circling the hoof parallel with the hair at the top of the hoof. This is the correct angle for the trimmed hoof to end up.

*PLEASE NOTE: I am not a veterinarian and have no veterinary training. It is not my intention to give medical advice. Before you follow any suggestion printed in this book that might be construed as medical advice, or administer any drug or vaccine, ALWAYS seek the advice of a qualified veterinarian.

The toes of the hoof grow faster than the heel. Because of this, many people tend to trim at the wrong angle - like this ------> This will cause the foot to roll backwards, forcing the pasterns to break down.

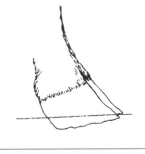

Start trimming slices off the hard side nail and the soft, white center to level out the hoof. Trim down until you can see the white change to pink. Trim the heel only down until it is level with the growth ring that the toe is on. The toe and heel should be at the same level.

There may be some little flaps coming out of the middle, between the hooves, these will need to be snipped off.

Then, using your carpenter's plane, and holding both toes together, so they will come out level, plane off the entire bottom of the hoof (including the heel) until it is level. If the hoof oozes little pin-pricks of blood, don't worry,

but definitely stop trimming for today. (It is not a bad idea to brush a little iodine on it before you set it down in the manure.) ♥

Sometimes, the heel is the part that seems to grow too fast, causing the goat to walk on the back of the hoof above the heel. In this case, be sure that you trim the hooves more often, and that you are not leaving the heel so long that the goat is walking on 'high heels'. If the hoof was drastically overgrown, and you didn't get it into the right shape, it is better to come back to it later than to make the goat lame, or risk serious bleeding and infection, by cutting too much at one time. Try again in one to three weeks. If it still isn't right, come back in another two or three weeks. Sometimes it takes a while to whip a goat's hooves into perfect shape.

Goat's hooves need to be trimmed regularly (and don't forget the bucks!).   That will mean different things depending on your ranch and conditions. If your goats have plenty of rocks to walk on, or are in a large herd that travels over many acres a day, you might be able to escape this chore for four to six months. Some people even build low platforms of rock and cement for the goats to play on to help them keep their hooves in shape. In most cases, when the goats are walking on grass or in pens, hooves should be trimmed every four to twelve weeks.

Vaccinating and Testing your goats

Vaccinations are part of a good management program. Beef raisers bring their cattle in at least twice a year for health and pregnancy checks, and to vaccinate. Keeping

---

♥ These wonderful hooves were drawn by Claudia Marcus Gurn of Mac Goats in Lincoln, California.

PLEASE NOTE: I am not a veterinarian and have no veterinary training. It is not my intention to give medical advice. Before you follow any suggestion printed in this book that might be construed as medical advice, or administer any drug or vaccine, ALWAYS seek the advice of a qualified veterinarian.

your animals healthy is the best way to keep them producing. Annual or biannual worming is an important part of a vaccination program.   C & D Perfringens antitoxin at birth and then toxoid boosters are the only way that we have to fight a universally lethal animal disease - Enterotoxemia. Tetanus shots are an obvious must.   Anything else that you have heard you should vaccinate for, may or may not be correct. The only way to know what is appropriate in your area is to talk to an experienced veterinarian or your county extension agent. When you are ready to vaccinate, always read the label carefully for dosage and injection instructions.

A subcutaneous injection (or sub-Q) is one that is given just under the skin. On a goat, this is usually done in the scruff of the neck just above the shoulder, or in the loose skin behind the front leg above the elbow.   To give a subcutaneous injection, pull the skin out away from the body a little. You will be able to feel where the skin is and where the muscle starts. Slide the needle in between the skin and the muscle.   (Always use 1 inch or shorter needles to avoid breaking them if the goat jumps.) Now pull back on the plunger to be sure you don't get any blood. If you get blood in your syringe, simply pull the needle out and try again in another spot. Do not try to put the blood back in the goat before you pull the needle out! It won't hurt him if you give him that blood back in another spot. If you get a little air when you pull back the plunger, you are doing OK. (If you get a lot of air, or your finger, you have gone all the way through both layers of skin, and you need to try again.)   Then push in the plunger to inject the medicine, and you're done!   If you give a lot of injections you will get used to it.

To give an intramuscular injection, you must find a good muscle. Most vets prefer to use the one in the back of the thigh.   Stand behind the goat (which has been restrained) and feel for the thick part of the back of the thigh. Use a short (3/4ths or 1 inch) needle to avoid hitting a nerve (there is a nerve that runs down the leg, and if you hit it you may cripple the goat).   Insert the needle into the muscle pointing towards the front of the goat. Pull back on the plunger (it is easy to hit blood here) and if you get no blood, go ahead and give the injection.

Another possible site for an intramuscular injection is the heavy muscle of the neck. If you would like to use this muscle, have your veterinarian show you how.

Blood testing is an easy way to check your herd for most diseases.   You can either take your animals to the veterinarian to have the blood drawn, or learn to do it yourself.   Drawing blood is not hard, if you have the stomach for it, and doing it yourself will cut mountains off your vet bill. I strongly suggest that you have someone show you the trick the first couple times, but here is one way to do it:

Just use a standard 3cc syringe with a normal 1" x 20 needle.   Get a couple of strong helpers to hold the goat. Shave the hair off one side of the goat's neck from the center to about 3 inches out.   Now feel the center of the neck for the voice box. From there, run your thumb along the skin towards the outside of the neck (about 1 1/2 to 2 inches) until you feel a rope like thing.   That is the vein. If you put your thumb on that vein you will notice a bulge develop a little ways above your thumb.   With your other hand, slide the needle into the bottom of that bulge in an almost straight up direction.   If you go through at too great an angle, you will go out the other side of the vein. If you go almost straight up, you will feel the resistance of the vein, then you will be in. The goat might jump a little, try to keep her still. Now you can take your thumb off of the vein and pull back on the plunger until you have the amount of blood you need.   (If you pull back on the plunger, and get air, remove the needle from the goat to expel the air. Do not take a chance on injecting air into a vein!) When you remove the needle from the goat's neck, put a cotton swab with alcohol on it over the hole and press it there for a minute to allow the blood to clot. You did it!

Now what? Put the blood into a standard blood tube with no additives in it.   They are usually a test tube looking thing with a red stopper in the top. You can buy these at

---

PLEASE NOTE: I am not a veterinarian and have no veterinary training. It is not my intention to give medical advice. Before you follow any suggestion printed in this book that might be construed as medical advice, or administer any drug or vaccine, ALWAYS seek the advice of a qualified veterinarian.

any reasonable medical supply house. (You may have to shop a bit for a "reasonable" one.) Now write the goat's name and/or number on the label on the tube, and put the tube in a small cup to hold it up, and put it in the fridge. After 5 hours or so you can send it to the lab for testing. If it is warm outside you may nccd to put a small cold pack in with it when you mail it.

Here are a few laboratories that may be able to process your blood sample. If there is not one listed in your area, try calling the one that is nearest to you. They probably know of another lab that is closer.

California Veterinary Diagnostic Lab System
West Health Sciences Drive
University of California - Davis
Davis, Calif. 95616
(916)752-7577

National Animal Disease Center
PO Box 70
Ames, Iowa 50010

Pan American Veterinary Laboratories
3921 Steck Ave
Austin, Texas 78759
(512)794-9657 Fax
(800)856-9655

Veterinary Diagnostic Laboratories
University of Minnesota
College of Veterinary Medicine
Carter and Gortner Aves.
St Paul, Minnesota 55108

Washington Animal Disease Diagnostic Laboratory
College of Veterinary Medicine
Washington State University
PO Box 2037
College Station/Bustad Hall, Rm 155-N
Pullman, Washington 99165-2037
(509)335-7424 Fax
(509)335-9696

Diagnostic Laboratory
Cornell University
College of Veterinary Medicine
Ithaca, New York 14853

Your Vet Kit

It is a good idea to have a kit, box or cabinet ready with some of the basic things you may need to take care of your goat's health needs. I would definitely include a Goat Veterinary book in this list. There are several good ones listed in the "Resources" chapter of this book. Here are a few other items that might come in handy:

20 X 1" needles
3cc syringes
antibacterial spray
antifungal spray
Betadine
C & D Perfringens antitoxin
C & D Perfringens toxoid
carpenter's plane for
    hoof trimming
hemostats
hoof trimming shears
Iodine 1%
iodine 7%
drench with propylene
glycol
a good probiotic

epinephrine
medical tape
penicillin
red top tubes
rubber surgical gloves
rubbing alcohol
scissors
stomach tube
sterile bandages
Tetanus antitoxin
Tetanus toxoid
vet wrap
veterinary thermometer
wormers
udder ointment (bag balm)

Measurement Converstions

1ml	=	15 drops	=	1cc
1 tsp.	=	1 gram	=	5 cc's
1Tbsp.	=	½ oz.	=	15 cc's
2Tbsp	=	1 oz.	=	30 cc's
1 pint	=	16 oz.	=	480 cc's [50]

PLEASE NOTE: I am not a veterinarian and have no veterinary training. It is not my intention to give medical advice. Before you follow any suggestion printed in this book that might be construed as medical advice, or administer any drug or vaccine, ALWAYS seek the advice of a qualified veterinarian.

NOTES:

11

Goat Ranching through the Year

In our modern world of urban sprawl and computerized everything, many people wander through life taking very little notice of the seasons. A person who lives in an apartment building, takes a bus to work and works in a high-rise, seldom has time to enjoy the change of summer to fall, or winter to spring. However, as soon as you move to the country and begin to ranch, the seasons suddenly become important. The seasons bring with them different tasks, different challenges and different triumphs.

A philosophical rancher will say to himself, "There is no bad season, and no bad weather!" The spring rains that make it difficult to keep the stock outdoors, are nurturing his pasture into glorious abundance. The lengthening days of summer that dry and burn the pasture, will soon start the physiological clock ticking toward breeding season in his animals. Even the freezing cold and snows of winter, that force him into the house, are giving the goats a time of slow paced retirement in which to finish their pregnancies. The rancher cannot change these things. He must accept the challenge of learning to understand the seasons and of adapting himself to work within their never-ending cycle.[51]

Picture 32: Spring is time to find those perfect kids.[*]

Spring is the Time to Buy Stock

In most areas of the world, kid goats are born in the early spring. When you are preparing to start your goat ranch, the best time to go shopping, as we discussed in Chapter 4, is the spring. You should start looking for spring kids as soon as they are well on their way to bouncing around the pasture, say March or April. Take a tour of the ranches on your list and choose your kids. Many times, this is the time of year breeders may decide which of their mature does will be staying for the next season, and which of them will be for sale. Occasionally, these does can be purchased in the spring with their kids by their side. I have always thought a comfortable way to start a herd is with kids and their mothers. That way, the move is easier for both.

---

[*] This picture donated by Hill Country Farms from Spicewood, Texas.

Once you have your new purchases picked out, and you have put down your deposit, it is time to go home and put the finishing touches on those fences and goat houses. Now you know what you are going to be bringing home, and can plan accordingly. Then, in late spring, when the new additions to the herd are ready to leave, you will have a well-thought-out environment for them to come home to.

Building Facilities in the Summer

It doesn't matter how long you have been building facilities; you are never quite finished. In the summer the kids are up and growing like weeds, the does are ready to be dried off, the pasture is still green enough to feed the herd, and you have time to work on the fences. Summer is the perfect time to put in that water line, electrical cable, extra goat house, etc.

I remember the first summer after we bought goats. My husband decided it was time to put in 1200 feet of water pipe and electrical conduit. We rented a 'ditcher', and were off and running. There were 12 inch wide by 3 foot deep ditches everywhere. Goats are smart animals, right? And very agile. You would think they could stay out of those ditches! We had kids running through them like tunnels, and does dropping into them on their butts. The older kids made a game of jumping into the ditch on one side and back out on the other side, then back in. Our pasture looked like we were raising jumping beans, popping spontaneously out of the ground! Summer is definitely the time for building.

Breeding in the Fall

As the summer heat finishes off the last of the pasture, the does start to come into heat, and the bucks begin to invent new routes of escape. Suddenly there is too much to do to finish those last building projects before winter.

Picture 33: As the summer heat finishes off the last of the pasture, the does start to come into heat.**

- This picture donated Kids-R-Us Goat Farm from Uvalde, Texas.
- This picture donated by Hill Country Farms from Spicewood, Texas.

Picture 34: and the bucks begin to invent new routes of escape. * *

- * This picture from Bowman Boer Ranch from Twin Falls, Idaho.
- * This picture from Caston Creek Ranch from Wister, Oklahoma.

You still have to move those young does to the other pasture, trim up all the hooves, learn to AI, go to two more goat shows, and "Can you <u>please</u> finish that fence?"

Where did the summer go? You had all that time! Now you are buying winter clothing. I have learned that ranching is much easier to do if you have the right clothing for the job. Around here, that means insulated overalls, insulated ranch jacket, Eskimo hat, insulated gloves, insulated work boots, and – no - let me guess – *insulated* long underwear!

Fall is also the time to be sure that you have enough feed for the coming winter. Take another look at the feed tables in Chapter 5, and refigure. Then be sure you have stored the feed in a way that will protect it from the weather. It took us years to learn that a cheap tarp meant we were feeding moldy hay in February!

Winter is a Time of Waiting

During the spring, summer and fall you are always under pressure to do one more thing, but here in the northwestern United States, winter is the time to take stock. The does are, hopefully, pregnant. The fences are as good as they are going to get for a while. The hay is under cover, and the goats are putting on an incredible winter coat.

Now is the time to 'count your chickens'. It is time to decide how many replacement does you are going to need, and whether you can expect to get them. It is also the time to read Chapter 9 and work on your flyers for spring.

Winter is time to bundle up in those insulated clothes and feed everyday, check on your pregnant mothers, and watch for colds. Spend some time out with the goats, listening to them breath, and watching them interact. Be sure you have sufficient heat in the water to keep it defrosted, and refill it every day. Even in the winter, you cannot afford to let down your guard. In the harsher conditions of the season, you can easily loose animals if you are not paying attention.

Picture 35: . I have learned that ranching is much easier to do if you have the right clothing for the job.[*]

---

[*] This picture from Bowman Boer Ranch in the Frozen Wastes of the North.

Spring Kidding and Sales

As the winter fades, too slowly, into spring the sap is rising in the rancher as well as the trees. We can't wait to be out in the sunshine with our goats! As spring rolls slowly into place, the goats will start to kid. Time for production! My very favorite time of year! I love to watch the kids being born. I just can't wait to see what they are going to look like, and fill in my spreadsheets (do you really think it's an obsession?), and then sit in the pasture and watch the new kids play and jump!

This is also the time to implement the advertising campaign you hatched in the solitude of winter. Finish printing the flyers, folding them, and addressing them. Flyers sent out in early spring will bring the best results, because other ranchers are now in the position you were in just a year ago. Be sure your kids are being creep fed, and your ranch looks presentable. It is time to reap some of the profit from your work and careful husbandry. Good luck and good ranching!

The Recipe Book

Goat meat is called Chevon or Cabrito. When dairy goat bloodlines are mixed with Boer, the meat loses some of the 'twang' and becomes a very mild meat much like veal or pork. We have already seen that goat meat is low in fat, it also easily lends itself to a huge range of spices and cuisine's. Here are an assortment of recipes for you to try. I think you may be surprised at the results!

Family Style Barbecues

Basic Barbecue Sauce

1 small onion, chopped
2 Tbsp. butter
½ Tbsp. cider vinegar
1 garlic, chopped
½ tsp. prepared mustard

Juice of 1 lemon
1 small bottle catsup
3 Tbsp. Worcestershire
1 Tbsp. brown sugar

Mix, stir, and bring to a boil, use as basting sauce and also table sauce.[52]

Baked Chevon with Barbecue Sauce

8 to 10 lbs. chevon
2 cups water
¼ tsp. salt
1 8-ounce can tomato sauce
2 Tbsp. butter
2 cloves garlic, minced
1 onion, minced
6 whole cloves

1 Tbsp. ground black
    pepper
1 Tbsp. sugar
2 Tbsp. vinegar
½ tsp. cumin
½ tsp. oregano
3 carrots, diced

Cut Chevon into serving pieces. Wash and dry the pieces. Place them in an open pan in a 350°F oven. Cook for 20 minutes using a meat thermometer, making sure internal temperature reaches 160°F. Prepare barbecue sauce. Simmer for 30 minutes. Baste Chevon with sauce every 15 to 20 minutes for 2 hours or until meat is very tender.[54]

Chevon Kabobs

1 Chevon shoulder roast, cut into 1 inch cubes
2 Tbsp. olive oil
¼ cup vinegar
½ tsp. dried oregano
1 clove garlic, finely chopped

1 tsp. salt
1 Tbsp. sugar
¼ tsp. pepper
4 small tomatoes,
    quartered

Arrange chevon in a shallow baking dish. In a jar with a tight lid, shake oil, vinegar, oregano, salt, sugar, pepper and garlic until well combined. Pour over chevon; refrigerate, covered, 3 hours, turning occasionally. Adjust grill so it is 4 inches above the coals. Remove chevon from the oil mixture. Arrange cubes alternatively with tomato quarters on skewers; brush with oil mixture. Frill Kabobs, turning and brushing several times with oil mixture, about 20 minutes, or until done.[53]

Roasts and Chops

Baked Chevon

1 shoulder or leg of Chevon
salt and pepper
1 cup apple cider vinegar
        mixed with
1 whole garlic, finely chopped

Hand rub Chevon with this mixture. Cover bottom of baking pan with sauce, add meat and water to measure ½ inch in pan. Bake at 350°F, 2 ½ to 3 hours. Turn and baste each hour.[54]

Southwest Leg of Chevon

1 leg of Chevon (5 to 7lbs), boned
1 cup wine or vinegar
1 cup vegetable oil
2 cloves garlic, whole
1 bay leaf, crumbled
1 tsp. rosemary
½ tsp. crushed pepper

2 tsp. salt
1 tsp. sage
3 large potatoes
3 onions
3 large chilies
2 garlic cloves,
        skin removed

Combine vinegar, oil and seasonings and pour over Chevon. Cover and marinate in refrigerator 12 to 24 hours, turning often. Remove meat, strain marinade and reserve. Quarter potatoes and onions and place in shallow roasting pan along with chilies and garlic and pour ¼ cup marinade over meat. Roast at 325°F for approximately 25 minutes per pound of meat. Baste with ¼ cup marinade every 20-30 minutes before carving. Serve with vegetables. Use drippings for gravy if desired.[54]

Cabrito Chops Jalapeno

4 Cabrito shoulder chops,
  1 in. thick, round bone
1 tsp. salt
½ tsp. ground pepper
½ tsp. ground cinnamon
1 Tbsp. prepared mustard

18 ounce crushed
  pineapple
  (in its own juice)
½ cup Jalapeno jelly
  (or apricot jam)
¼ cup fresh
  lemon juice

Sprinkle Cabrito shoulders with a mixture of salt, pepper, and cinnamon. Combine remaining ingredients in small saucepan. Bring to a boil, stirring until jelly is melted. Broil or grill chops 4 inches from heat source, 8-10 minutes on each side. Spoon sauce on meat last 5 minutes of cooking time.[54]

Honey Grilled Shoulder of Cabrito

1 shoulder of Cabrito,
  boned & rolled (3 ½ to 4 lbs.)
2 Tbsp. lemon juice
1/3 cup honey
½ cup dry white wine
½ cup finely chopped fresh mint
  or 1 Tbsp. dried mint

2 Tbsp. grated lemon
  peel

1 tsp. salt
¼ tsp. ground pepper
½ cup finely chopped
  onion

Place Cabrito meat in a glass dish. Combine remaining ingredients and pour over Cabrito. Cover and refrigerate several hours or overnight. Place Cabrito on spit over hot coals and grill 1 to 1 ½ hours. Brush occasionally with marinade. Any leftover marinade may be heated and served over sliced Cabrito.[54]

Chevon Netted Roast

2 ½ to 3 lbs. Cabrito roast
salt and pepper to taste
¾ cup water

One envelope onion &
  mushroom soup mix

Rinse Cabrito roast under tap water. Pat dry. Salt and pepper on all sides. Place roast in large stew pot or small Dutch oven that has been sprayed with non-stick coating or oiled. Mix one packet of onion and mushroom soup mix with ¾ cup of water; pour into pan with roast. Bring to a simmer, reduce heat, and cook approximately 2 hours. Turn roast once about halfway through cooking time. Slice roast and serve onion-mushroom mixture as gravy.[54]

Intercontinental Main Dishes

Hawaiian Chevon Mini-Kabobs

1 Lb. boneless leg of Chevon cut into ¾ in. cubes	3 slices bacon, (cut in 1in. pieces)
1 cup Italian dressing	1 14 ounce can
1 clove garlic, minced	pineapple chunks
¼ cup melted butter	(cut in half)

Combine cubed meat, dressing and garlic in a shallow glass dish and marinate for 1 hour or overnight in the refrigerator. Alternate cubes of Chevon, bacon and pineapple on mini-skewers or round toothpicks. Brush with melted butter. Broil 5-8 inches from heat source for 5 minutes. Serve hot.[54]

Chevon de Vermicelli (with noodles)

1 ½ Lb. Chevon, cubed	½ Tbsp. whole black pepper
1 Tbsp. cumin seed	
2 Tbsp. vegetable oil	3 small garlic cloves
1 small onion, diced	5 to 6 oz vermicelli
1 green bell pepper, diced	2 fresh tomatoes, diced

Cut Chevon into bite-size cubes and brown in skillet with oil until well done (approximately 20 to 30 minutes). Combine onion and bell pepper and set aside. In blender, grind cumin seed, black pepper, and garlic cloves until pulverized. Combine spices with Chevon and vegetables; mix well. Add vermicelli and enough water to cover entire mixture and then add diced tomatoes. Cover and bring to a slow simmer. Cook approximately 15 minutes or until vermicelli is tender. Do not stir until ready to serve.[54]

Chevon and Vegetable Casserole

1 10 ounce pkg. frozen lima beans
1 ½ cup thinly sliced carrots
1 cup boiling water
1 ½ lbs. ground Chevon
1 ½ tsp. salt
2 Tbsp. chopped onion
1 Tbsp. vegetable oil
2 Tbsp. grated Parmesan cheese

1 10 ½ ounce can
   cream of mushroom
   soup
1/3 cup vegetable
   liquid
¼ tsp. thyme
6 tomato slices, ¾ in.
½ tsp. salt

Add lima beans and carrots to boiling water. Cook covered until tender, about 15 to 20 minutes. Drain and save cooking liquid. Preheat oven to 350°F. Cook ground Chevon and onion in oil until Chevon is lightly brown and onion is transparent. Pour off drippings. Add soup, vegetable liquid, vegetables, salt and thyme. Mix well and pour into a 2-quart casserole. Arrange tomato slices on top of mixture. Sprinkle with salt and cheese. Bake 35 to 40 minutes.[54]

Chevon Riblets in Barbecue Sauce

4 lbs. Chevon riblets
8 oz. can pineapple chunks
1 lemon, thinly sliced
1/3 cup chopped onion
¾ cup chili sauce
2 Tbsp. Worcestershire sauce

2 Tbsp. brown sugar
2 Tbsp. vinegar
1 tsp. salt
¼ tsp. ginger
1/8 tsp. crushed red
   pepper

Brown riblets on all sides in a large frypan. Drain pineapple chunks, set aside juice. Add pineapple chunks and lemon slices to riblets. Combine remaining ingredients with reserved pineapple juice and pour over riblets. Cover and simmer 1 ½ hours or until tender. Skim off melted fat before serving. Serves 6.[54]

Chevon Fry

Marinate Chevon, in the refrigerator, in this mixture for 24 hours:

1 medium minced onion	1 Tbsp. parsley
6 whole pepper corns	2 cups white wine
1 Tbsp. salt	1 tsp. paprika

Take chevon out of marinating mixture. Dredge in seasoned flour (1 cup flour, 2 Tbsp. Paprika, 2 tsp. each pepper and salt). Saute chevon in hot oil, turning with tongs until thoroughly brown. Drain on paper towels.

1 large onion, sliced	1 green pepper, sliced
3 Tbsp. olive oil	1 can cream of
1 small can tomato puree	mushroom soup
salt and pepper	1 oz. Sherry

Put chevon on a cookie sheet and bake in 250° oven for 25 to 30 minutes or until done. In another pan, saute onion and green pepper in olive oil for 5 minutes. Remove onion and pepper and put aside. Add 2 Tbsp. of the seasoned flour mixture to the oil and stir over gentle heat until smooth and brown. Add soup and puree, simmer for 5 minutes. Return onion and pepper to sauce and simmer for 15 minutes. Add salt and pepper to taste, add sherry. Serve with chevon.[53]

Chevon and Artichoke Casserole

2 Tbsp. salad oil	1 ½ tsp. curry
¼ tsp. pepper	powder
2 lbs. cubed Chevon	
2 medium onions, sliced	½ lb. zucchini, sliced
1 clove crushed garlic	1 pkg. frozen
1 cup raw white rice	artichoke hearts
1 lb. potatoes, sliced thin	2 cans (1 lb. Size)
4 tsp. salt	tomatoes, undrained
chopped parsley	

Preheat oven to 350°F. In hot oil, saute chevon cubes until well browned. Remove chevon. Add onion and garlic to drippings, and saute until golden. Return chevon cubes to skillet, mix well. In 3 quart casserole, place in layers, 1/3 of the meat mixture, rice, potatoes, salt, curry, pepper, zucchini, artichoke hearts, and tomatoes. Repeat all layers twice. Bake uncovered 2 hours or more. Sprinkle with parsley. Serves 6 to 8.[53]

Curry Cabrito

2 Tbsp. oil
1 medium onion, chopped
1/3 cup chopped celery
½ cup chopped green pepper
1 pared apple, thinly sliced
2 tsp. curry powder

Melt butter in large frying pan, add onion, celery, green pepper, and apple sliced; cook until onion is tender. Stir occasionally. Gently stir in spices. Cook over low heat, stirring until mixture is hot. Gradually add broth, heat to boiling, stirring constantly. Cook for one minute. Stir in meat; heat thoroughly. Serve over hot rice.[52]

Curried Chevon

1lb Chevon
salt to taste
3 oz butter
2 Tbsp. minced onion
2 Tbsp. finely cut celery
2 Tbsp. diced apples

1 Tbsp. flour
1 Tbsp. curry powder
2 ripe tomatoes,
  stewed and strained
1 ½ cup water

Cut meat into 1-inch squares; salt meat and sauté in butter. Add onion and apples; sauté thoroughly. Sprinkle mixture with flour and curry powder and cook until flour colors. Add strained tomatoes and water, cover saucepan and let cook slowly until done. Serve with steamed rice.[54]

Cabrito with Mexican Rice (Arroz con Cabrito)

Prepare 1 cup of uncooked rice according to package directions. While the rice cooks, prepare the following ingredients:

1 medium onion,
  peeled & chopped
½ tsp. salt
1 medium green bell pepper,
  seeded and chopped
1 8-ounce can tomato sauce
1 lbs. ground Cabrito

1 heaping Tbsp. chili
  powder
½ tsp. cumin
¼ tsp. oregano
1 Tbsp. oil

Saute onion and bell pepper in 1 Tbsp. oil; then add ground Cabrito and cook until nearly done, stirring and breaking up with a wooden spoon. Add spices, mix well, and then add tomato sauce, stirring vigorously. Add drained, cooked rice, mixed well and let stand for 15 minutes before serving.[54]

Enchilada Casserole

1 large onion, chopped
2 Tbsp. oil
1 can hot enchilada sauce
2 lbs. lean ground Cabrito
½ LB mild cheddar cheese
1 can cream of chicken soup

1 can cream of
  mushroom soup
12 corn tortillas
1 4-ounce can green
  chilies, or 3 large
  chilies

Saute onions in 2 Tbsp. oil in large skillet. Add meat and brown for a few minutes, breaking up with a spoon. Add chilies, soups, and enchilada sauce, mixing well. Cook until thoroughly heated. Cut each tortilla in 8 pieces and arrange half in a layer in the bottom of a 13x9x2 inch baking dish. Cover with a layer of meat mixture. Sprinkle half of the grated cheese on top of the meat. Repeat with the second layer. Bake at 350°F for 35 to 45 minutes.[54]

Stir-Fry Chevon with Green Onions

2/3 lb. chevon (loin or leg), cut into thin slices
2 Tbsp. sesame of safflower oil
12 green onions, cut into 1 inch lengths

Marinade # 1	Marinade # 2
½ tsp. garlic powder	3 Tbsp. soy sauce
2 Tbsp. soy sauce	½ tsp. sugar
½ Tbsp. sugar	½ tsp. black pepper
2 Tbsp. rice wine	4 Tbsp. water
2 Tbsp. cornstarch	

Cut meat into uniform 1/8-inch slices, 1 ½ to 2 inches long. Place meat in a sealable bag; add marinade # 1 and shake to coat thoroughly. Refrigerate at least 1 hour, shaking at least once. When ready to cook, stir-fry meat in sesame or safflower oil, stirring often. Add marinade # 2 and green onions. Continue to stir-fry until thoroughly hot; serve over warm rice.[54]

Sweet and Sour Chevon

1 cup chopped onion	2/3 cup brown sugar
1 cup diced celery	¾ cup white wine
½ cup chopped green pepper	½ cup orange juice
1 cup sliced fresh mushrooms	¼ cup catsup
1 lg. clove garlic, finely chopped	1 Tbsp. vinegar
2 Tbsp. vegetable oil	1 Tbsp.
2 Tbsp. flour	Worcestershire
1 Tbsp. prepared Dijon mustard	2 cups hot cooked
1 ½ lb. boneless Chevon	rice
¼ cup Parmesan cheese	

In a large skillet, sauté onion, celery, green pepper, mushrooms, and garlic in vegetable oil. Pour into a shallow baking dish. Tenderize meat and cut into chucks. Place over vegetables. Prepare sauce by combining brown sugar, wine, mustard; pour over Chevon and vegetables. Simmer for 1 hour. Remove excess grease from liquid in pan. In small bowl, combine flour and ¼ cup water. Gradually add a small amount of the hot liquid from the baking dish; stir until smooth. Pour flour mixture into saucepan and cook, stirring, over medium heat about 5 minutes or until thick. Sprinkle with cheese. Serve over hot rice.[52]

Texas Ranch Style Gumbo

2 ½ lbs. Boneless Chevon
¼ cup all-purpose flour

1 tsp. dried whole thyme
½ tsp. salt
¼ tsp. pepper
3 Tbsp. butter
¾ cup chopped green onion

1 large green pepper
3 large tomatoes,
  chopped
1 bay leaf
2 cups chicken broth
1 pkg. frozen okra
½ tsp. hot sauce
6 cups hot cooked
  rice

Trim excess fat from steak and cut into 1 inch cubes. Combine flour, thyme, salt, and pepper; dredge meat in flour mixture. Heat butter and oil in Dutch oven; add meat and cook until browned on all sides. Remove meat, reserving drippings in Dutch oven. Add onion and green pepper to reserved drippings, sauté until tender. Stir in meat and remaining ingredients except rice. Cover and simmer 1 ½ hours. Remove bay leaf and serve over hot rice.[52]

Chevon Teriyaki

2 lbs. boneless Chevon
¼ cup sherry wine
1/3 cup soy sauce
1/3 cup canned chicken broth

1 Tbsp. sugar
2 Tbsp. cornstarch
1 Tbsp. cold water

Trim meat of excess fat and cut into 12 pieces. Pound meat slightly with a meat pounder. To make teriyaki sauce, blend together sherry, soy sauce, and broth. Set aside ¼ cup of sauce, and then marinate meat in remaining sauce for 1 hour. To make teriyaki glaze, combine the sugar with the ¼ cup of reserved sauce, and then heat gently (do not boil). Dissolve cornstarch in water, stir into hot glaze and cook over medium heat until thick. Skewer 4 to 5 pieces of meat onto each bamboo skewer. Cook over high heat on pit or hibachi. Grill for 5 minutes on each side. Dip into teriyaki glaze after cooking, and serve with rice and mixed vegetable salad.[54]

Tortilla Spicy Cabrito

2 cups cooked Cabrito,
   shredded
 6 small tomatoes, chopped
8 small flour tortillas
3 Tbsp. white vinegar
1 to ½ Jalapeno pepper,
   seeded and diced
 ¼ cup sour cream
1 Tbsp. finely chopped onion
½ tsp. crushed red pepper
1 Tbsp. finely snipped cilantro
1/8 tsp. garlic powder

½ tsp. ground cumin
½ tsp. dried
   coriander

1 medium avocado,
   sliced
½ cup shredded
   cheese
¾ cup shredded
   lettuce
½ tsp. dried oregano

Combine 1 cup tomatoes, vinegar, jalapeno pepper, onion, cilantro and garlic powder in small saucepan to make a salsa. Cook over medium heat for 5 minutes and chill. In large frypan, combine cabrito, remaining tomatoes, oregano, red pepper, cumin and coriander. Cook over medium heat 8 to 10 minutes or until cabrito is thoroughly heated. Divide cabrito and tomato mixture among tortillas. Top each tortilla with avocado, cheese and lettuce. Roll up tortillas and serve with sour cream and chilled salsa. Makes 4 servings.[54]

Veggie Chevon Rolls

20 oz Chevon
2 tsp. prepared
   horseradish sauce

1 large dill pickle,
   quartered lengthwise
2 cups vegetable juice cocktail

1 medium carrot,
   chopped
1 celery stick,
   chopped
1 medium zucchini,
   chopped

In covered saucepan, place vegetable steamer over simmering water. Steam carrot and celery for 5 minutes. Add zucchini and continue to steam for 5 to 7 minutes, or until crisp and tender, and drain. Place each slice of Chevon between two pieces of waxed paper. With a meat mallet, pound Chevon until about ¼ inch thick. Spread ½ tsp. prepared horseradish sauce on each Chevon slice.

Divide pickle, carrot, celery and zucchini for each slice. Roll each Chevon slice from the short end and secure with a wooden pick. Place rolls in a 8x8-inch glass baking dish. Pour vegetable juice over rolls. Cover with foil and bake at 325⁰ for 50 to 60 minutes, or until Chevon is tender. Skim off sauce and serve. Makes 4 servings.[54]

Chili and Stews

Artichoke Stew

1 clove garlic	2 onions, sliced
2 ½ lbs. Chevon stew meat	1 cup burgundy wine
½ tsp. dill	1 can beef consume
1 pkg. artichoke hearts, frozen	18 mushrooms, medium
1 pkg. unbaked dinner rolls	Parmesan Cheese
Butter	

Brown onions and garlic in oil. Take onions out of oil and put aside. Brown stew meat in the same oil (Flour meat in seasoned flour first). Add the onion mixture, wine, Consume and dill. Cook until the meat is tender (about 1.5 hours).

In the meantime, cook the artichoke hearts one minute less than the package directs, put aside. Sauté mushrooms, put aside. Put the meat in a Casserole dish, add the artichokes and the mushrooms. Arrange the dinner rolls like a crown around the top of the Casserole dish. Bake in 400⁰ oven until 5 minutes before the rolls are done. Butter the tops of the rolls. Sprinkle with Parmesan Cheese and bake until rolls are done.[53]

Chevon Chili

2 Tbsp. cooking oil	1 Tbsp. salt
2 cups chopped onions	3 lbs. lean ground
1 Tbsp. ground oregano	Chevon
½ c + 2 Tbsp. chili powder	
2 Tbsp. ground cumin	½ cup flour
1 tsp. garlic powder	8 cups boiling water

In a heavy pot, saute' onions in cooking oil, add oregano, cumin, garlic powder, and salt. Stir and saute' until onion is almost clear, then add ground meat and cook and stir until crumbly and almost gray. Add chili power and then flour, stirring vigorously until thoroughly blended. Lastly, add boiling water, bring mixture to a boil, and simmer for not more than one hour. Seasonings may be adjusted to individual taste; serve beans as a side dish.[54]

Chevon Stew

8 lbs. chevon	¼ cup vegetable oil
3 Tbsp. salt	(to brown meat)
¾ cup flour	¾ cup vegetable oil
3 large tomatoes,	(to brown flour)
peeled & diced	8 cups cold tap water
1 large onion,	1 whole green bell
sliced in rings	pepper sliced
2 tsp. ground cumin	10 medium garlic
1 tsp. dried oregano	cloves pressed
1 ½ tsp. ground pepper	

Cut meat into ½" cubes. In a large Dutch oven heat ¼ cup oil at medium high heat. Place meat and salt in heated oil and cook for about 60 min., stirring occasionally. Remove from heat and set aside. In a large skillet heat ¾ cup oil, add flour and brown well. Turn off heat and add water (1 cup at a time) to make gravy. Add vegetables and spices to meat and mix well. Simmer 25 to 35 minutes at medium heat till meat and vegetables are tender. [54]

Glorious Chevon Stew

2 Tbsp. vegetable oil	A handful of mushrooms
2 lbs. Chevon stew meat	3 medium carrots
salt and pepper	10 small onions
1 clove garlic	1 tsp. sugar
2 Tbsp. Flour	5 medium potatoes
2 cups water	3 Tbsp. Sherry wine
2 Tbsp. Tomato paste	1 cup cooked peas

1 bouquet garni (To make a garni, tie together with clean string, 2 onion slices, 1 carrot, 1 stalk celery, 1 bay leaf and a few sprigs parsley.)

Preheat oven to 325°F. In skillet, heat oil until it is very hot. Sprinkle meat with salt and pepper, and brown in skillet on all sides. Drain off fat. Lower heat and add crushed garlic, and sprinkle flour over chevon. Cook slowly until all the flour has been absorbed. Stir in 2 cups of water and tomato paste. Bring to a boil. Pour meat mixture into a 3 quart casserole dish. Add the bouquet garni. Cover and bake 30 minutes in the oven, then remove garni.

Next, saute fresh mushrooms about 3 minutes in a little butter or olive oil. Add quartered carrots and onions to the skillet and sprinkle sugar over the vegetables. Cook only long enough to make them glisten from the sugar. Combine all vegetables and any meat liquid to the meat in the casserole dish. Bake 1 hour, or until tender. Stir in wine and peas. Serves 6.[53]

Meals for Large Crowds

Seminar Barbecue

About 30 to 45 Chevon chops
52 ounce bottle of Bulls Eye (or your favorite) Barbecue Sauce
1 Can Coke or Pepsi
About 4 shakes of Tobasco Sauce
A large throw-away turkey roasting pan

Arrange chops two layers deep in turkey pan.   Mix together entire bottle of Barbecue Sauce, Coke or Pepsi and Tobasco Sauce. Pour sauce over chops. Cover with aluminum foil. Bake in 300° oven for about 2 hours or until chops are done. The meat should come off the bone easily. Carefully remove from the oven, drain off some of the liquid, and serve with potato salad, chips, etc.

→   I stumbled on this quick and delicious recipe when I was under too much pressure to get the Seminar off the ground. I made 90 chops for 30 people, and they were picking through the empty pans!

Barbecued Chevon-Texas Style

20 pounds Chevon	1 Tbsp. black pepper
1 cup salt	1 Tbsp. cumin
1 jalapeno, sliced	
2 cups sugar (to taste)	1 tsp. salt
1 cup prepared mustard	1 tsp. black pepper
½ cup apple cider vinegar	

Mix salt, jalapeno, black pepper, and cumin; sprinkle meat generously. Top with jalapeno slices. Cook slowly on grill 2 hours (or less, depending on cut of meat). Be sure meat is well above fire (at least 20 to 24 inches). Meat may be brushed with cooking oil occasionally to prevent dryness. Prepare sauce while meat cooks. At least 30 minutes before removing from fire, brush meat with sauce so it will "set." Continue cooking and turn the meat often, brushing on sauce at every turn.

(From Society for Range Management Cowboy Cookbook)[54]

An Important Note about Chevon:

Chevon, or cabrito, will spoil very quickly if left out of the fridge. Tell your butcher not to let the scraps, that he is going to make into ground meat, sit out very long. Also, do not marinate outside the refrigerator.

Resources

Associations and Registries

American Boer Goat Assoc.
232 W Beauregard, Suite 104
San Angelo, TX 76903
915-486-2242

American Dairy Goat Assoc.
P.O. Box 865
Spindale, NC 28160
828-286-3801

American Goat Society
RR 1, Box 56
Esperance, NY 12066-9704
518-875-6708

American Kiko Goat Assoc.
P.O. Box 186
Lakeland, GA 31635-9998
912-244-6058

American Meat Goat Assoc.
P.O. Box 1321
Sonora, TX 76950
915-387-6100

American Tenn. Fainting Goat
Assoc.
RR 4, Box 4100
Houlton, ME 04730

Australian Boer Goat Breeders'
Assoc.
RMB 4554, Rawlings Rd
Newry, Vic 3859
Australia
051-451367

Boer Goat Assoc. of Australia
LTD
P.O. Box 304
Belair, SA 5052
Australia
08-410-0233

Boer Goat Breeders' Assoc. of
South Africa
P.O. Box 282
Somerset East 5850
Republic of South Africa
0424-32139

Canadian Boer Goat Assoc.
Box 1136
Glenwood, Alberta TOK 2R0
403-626-3280

Canadian Goat Society
2417 Holly Lane
Ottawa, Ontario K1V 0M7
613-731-9894

European Boer Goat Assoc.
The Old Dairy
Foothill Bishop
Salisbury, Wiltshire SP3 55H
United Kingdom
74-782-0391 Fax

International Boer Goat Assoc.
Rt. 3, Box 111
Bonham, TX 75418
903-640-4242

International Fainting Goat
Assoc.
3450 320th Street
Terril, IA 51364
712-853-6372

International Goat Assoc.
1015 S. Louisiana Street
Little Rock, AR 72202
501-376-6836

Mohair Council of America
P.O. Box 5337
San Angelo, TX 76902
915-655-3161

British Goat Society
34-36 Fore Srteet
Bovey Tracey
Newton Abbott, Devon TQ13
9AD
0626-833168

New Zealand Boer Goat Br.
Assoc.
P.O. Box 97155
South Aukland Mail Center
New Zealand
09-267-4857

The IBGA (A Boer Goat
Registry Association)
P.O. Box 663
Spicewood, TX 78669
877-640-4242

Catalogues and Venders

American Livestock Supply
P.O. Box 8441
Madison, WI 53708
800-356-0700

Caprine Supply
33001 West 83rd St.
P.O. Box Y
DeSoto, KS 66018
800-646-7736 (Phone orders)
913-585-1191

D.M. Peifer Supplies
P.O. Box 503
Herndon, PA 17830
717-758-8464

Hoegger Supply Co.
P.O.Box 331
Fayetteville, GA 30214
770-461-4129

Jeffers Vet Supply
P.O. Box 948
West Plains, MO 65775
800-533-3377

Sydell Inc. (Equipment)
46935 SD Hwy 50
Burbank. SD 57010-9605
605-624-4538

KV Vet Supply Company
3190 North Rd
David City, Nebraska 68632
800-423-8211

Nasco
901 Janesville Ave.
Fort Atkinson, WI 53538-0901
920-563-2446
and
4825 Stoddard Rd.
Modesto, CA 95356-9318
209-545-1600

Omaha Vaccine Company
3030 L St. PO Box 7228
Omaha, NE 68107
800-367-4444

PBS Livestock Health
P.O. Box 9101
Canton, OH 44711-9101
800-321-0235

Agristore
Meadow Mate Products
94 E. Bremer
Waverly, IA 50677
319-352-3602

Books

Goat Health Handbook
By Dr. Thomas Thedford

Raising Milk Goats the Modern
By Jerry Belanger

**Goat Medicine
By Mary C. Smith and David
M. Sherman
Lea & Febiger Publishing

The Goatkeeper's Veterinary Book
By Peter Dunn
Farming Press

Your Goats
By Gail Damerow

Goat Breeds of the World
By Valerie Porter

Caprine Cooking
By Mary Jane Toth

Diseases and Disorders of
Sheep and Goats
By Karl A. Linklater
Wolfe Publishing

Goat Keeping 101
By Caprine Supply, 1998

Goat Husbandry
By David Mackenzie

Nutrient Requirements of
Goats
Subcommittee on Animal Nut.
National Academy Press, 1981

Basic Butchering of Livestock
And Game
By John Mettler, Jr.

Angora Goats the N. Way
By Susan Black Drummond

Tan Your Hide!
By Phyllis Hobson

Artificial Insemination
Handbook
Magnum Semen Works
2200 Albert Hill Road
Hampstead, MO 21074

Sheep and Goat Science
By M.E. Ensminger and R.O.
Parker
Ensinger Publishing

** This is a very good resource for goat breeders with excellent
explanations of health and disease problems in understandable
language. I highly recommend it.

Magazines and Newspapers

Boerbok Nuus (Boer Goat News)
Boer Breeders' Assoc. of S.A.
P.O. Box 282
Somerset-Oos/East 5850
Republic of South Africa
0424-32130

Ranch and Rural Living Mag.
P.O. Box 2678
San Angelo, TX 76902
915-655-4434

Countryside & Small Stock
Journal

The Goat Magazine
2268 County Rd. 285
Gillett, TX 78166
830-789-4268

United Caprine News

American Livestock Magazine
PO Box 931
Gatesville, TX 76528
254-248-1905

Goat Tracks
c/o Ellen McMaster
37719 SE 35th Street
Washougal, WA 92671
360-835-8285

Goat Rancher Magazine
731 Sandy Branch Road
Sarah, MS 38665
601-562-9529

The Goat Farmer
130 Maunu Road
Whangarei, New Zealand
0-9-438-0335
        and
Narrakup Chaney's Rd
Grenfell NSW 2810
Australia

Rocky Mountain Livestock
Journal
Twin Publishing Co., Inc.
PO Box 1378.
Mesilla, NM 88046-1378
505-524-1012

The Exotic and Livestock
Magazine
1302 W. North Ave.
Lampasas, TX 76550
512-556-6297

Small Farm Today
3903 W Ridge Trail Rd
Clark, MO 65243-9525
800-633-2535

About the Author

Gail Bowman raises goats near Twin Falls, Idaho with her husband, David, and their 5 children. Gail has a Bachelor's Degree in Education, and many years of teaching and writing experience. When she first started raising goats, Gail found reliable advice and information, not through good books, but through breeders with years of experience. She began to collect this wisdom in files and notes jotted during emergencies, visits and conversations. In 1997, Gail began writing humorous and informational articles about goat husbandry for several magazines. Although this is her first full sized book, Gail is already working on a children's series about 'Sera', the goat kid we have met on the title page of each chapter in "Raising Meat Goats for Profit".

Index

Bibliography and Endnotes

[1] Casey, N.H., and W.A. Van Niekerk. "Boer Goat I. Origin, Adaptability, Performance Testing, Reproduction and Milk Production." Small Rumin. Res., 1:291-302

[2] Campbell, Quentin Peter. "The Boer Goat – Outstanding Producer of Red Meat from Low Quality Grazing"

[3] Thian Hor Teh and Terry Gipson. "Establishing a Chevon Industry: The Boer Goat (Part I)"

[4] International Boer Goat Association South African Boer Goat Breed Standards" a publication of the International Boer Goat Association, Bonham, Texas. Feb 1997

[5] "History, development and Characteristics of Kiko Goats: An Overview" a publication of Goatex Group LLC, Fendalton, Christchurch, New Zealand.

[6] Kiko Goat Breed Standard" a publication of Kiko Goat Regisrty North America, Kerrville, Texas. Oct 1994

[7] "ATFGA" a publication of the American Tennessee Fainting Goat Association.

[8] "International Fainting Goat Breed Standard" a publication of the International Fainting Goat Association

[9] Dillman, Terry. "Meat Goat Producers can't keep up with demand." Capital Press, November 27, 1998

[10] USDA Handbook, H&B Bulletin 72

[11] Pinkerton, Frank and Lynn Harwell. "Tips for enhancing profitability of Southeastern meat goat enterprise." The Goat Rancher Magazine, April 1998

[12] Hansen, Alice. "Mingling livestock can offer benefits." Capital Press, 1998

[13] Fires, Alan J. "Meat Goat Judging Workshop" The Winkler Country 4-H Goat Manuel, 1993

[14] Pinkerton, Frank. "Procurement of Foundation Stock."

[15] Subcommittee on Goat Nutrition, Nutrient Requirements of Goats, National Academy Press, Washington D.C., 1981

[16] Bundy, Clarence E. and Ronald V. Diggins. Livestock and Poultry Production, Prentice-Hall, 1968, p. 696

[17] Artificial Insemination Handbook, Magnum Semen Works, 1986

[18] Belanger, Jerry. Raising Milk Goats the Modern Way, Storey Communications Press, 1990

[19] From Wess Hallman, from Oneonta, Alabama.

[20] Grotelueschen, Dale M., et al. "Type C Enterotoxemia in Young Calves." Cooperative Extension Institue of Agriculture and Natural Resources, U of Nebraska, September 1996, pubs@unlvm.unl.edu

[21] Ayers, J.L. "Enterotoxemia." Pennsylvania State U., Extension Goat Handbook, June 1992

[22] Homeyer, Fred C. "Some thoughts about Goat Toys and Floppy Kid Syndrome." Meat Goat News, February 1997. P.16

[23] De la Concha, Andres. "Finding a Cure for 'Floppy' Kid Syndrome." The Goat Farmer, June 1997, p.42

[24] Gnam, Rene. Direct Mail Workshop, Prentice Hall, 1989

[25] Sherman, David M. "Unexplained Weight Loss in Sheep and Goats." The Veterinary Clinics of North America, Nov 1983 Vol 5, Num 3 p.571-590

[26] Machen, Rick, Frank Craddock, Tom Craig, and Tom Fuchs. "A Haemonchus Contortus Management Plan for Sheep and Goats in Texas" Texas Agricultural Extension Service.

[27] Fubini, Susan L., and S. Gordon Campbell. "External Lumps on Sheep and Goats." The Veterinary Clinics of North America, Nov 1983 Vol 5, Num 3 p.457-476

[28] Craddock, Frank. "Coccidiosis." Texas Agricultural Extension Service.

[29] Smith, Mary. "Foot Problems in Goats." The Veterinary Clinics of North America, Nov 1983 Vol 5, Num 3 p.489-490

[30] East, Nancy E. "Pregnancy Toxemia, Abortions, and Periparturient Diseases." The Veterinary Clinics of North America, Nov 1983 Vol 5, Num 3 p.601-618

[31] Blood, D, J. A. Henderson, O. M. Radostits. Veterinary Medicine, Edition 5. Philadelphia, Lea and Febiger, 1979.

[32] Rowe, Joan Dean, and Nancy E. East. "Risk Factors for Transmission and Methods for Control of Caprine Arthritis-Encephalitis Virus Infection." The Veterinary Clinics of North America, Mar 1997, Vol 13, #1

[33] East, Nancy E. "Diseases of the Udder." The Veterinary Clinics of North America, Nov 1983 Vol 5, Num 3 p.591-600

[34] Greenwood, P. L., R. N. North, and P. D. Kirkland. "Prevalence, spread and control of Caprine Arthritis-Encephalitis Virus in dairy goats in herd in New South Wales," Aust Vet J 72:341, 1995

[35] Oliver, R. E., R. A. McNiven, and A. F. Julian, et al. "Experimental infection of sheep and goats with Caprine Arthritis-Encephalitis Virus." NZ Vet 30:158, 1982

[36] Ellis, T. M., H. Carman and W. F. Robinson, et a;. "The effect of colostrum-derived antibody on neo-natal transmission of Caprine Arthritis-Encephalitis Virus Infection." Aust Vet J 63:242, 1986

[37] Rimstad, E., N. East, and E. DeRock, et al. "Detection of antibody to Caprine Arthritis-Encephalitis Virus using recombinant gag proteins." Arch Virol 134:345, 1994

[38] Ashfaq, M. K., and S. G. Cambell. "Caseous lymphadenitis." In Gall, C. (ed.): Goat Production, London, Acedemic Press, 1981

[39] Smith, Mary C. and David M. Sherman. Goat Medicine. Lea & Febinger Publishing

[40] Blackwell, T. E. "Enteritis and Diarrhea." The Veterinary Clinics of North America, Nov 1983 Vol 5, Num 3 p.557-570

[41] Smith, Mary C. "Dermatologic Diseases of Sheep and Goats." The Veterinary Clinics of North America, Nov 1983 Vol 5, Num 3 p.449-455

[42] Sherman, D. M., and S. B. Guss. "Johne's Disease." Extension Goat Handbook, June 1992

[43] Haynes, Bruse N. Keeping Livestock Healthy, Garden Way Publishing, p.174-175, 187-189 & 278-279

[44] Brewer, Barbara D. "Neurologic Disease of Sheep and Goats." The Veterinary Clinics of North America, Nov 1983 Vol 5, Num 3 p.677-700

[45] Subcommittee on Goat Nutrition, Nutrient Requirements of Goats, National Academy Press, Washington D.C., 1981, p. 23

[46] Kimberling, Cleon V, and Kristin S. Arnold. "Diseases of the Urinary System of Sheep and Goats." The Veterinary Clinics of North America, Nov 1983 Vol 5, Num 3 p.637-653

[47] Cordes, Tim. "Precautions for horses diagnosed with Vesicular Stomatitis." 1998, tcordes@aphis.usda.gov

[48] Mead, Robert. "Blistering Disease Again Detected in Horses." June 26, 1997 Washington State Department of Agriculture.

[49] Robinson, Robert A.. "Respiratory Diseases of Goats." The Veterinary Clinics of North America, Nov 1983 Vol 5, Num 3 p.539-555

[50] Caprine Supply's Goatkeeping 101, 1998, p. 177

[51] Seymour, John. The Self Sufficient Gardener. Doubleday & Company, 1979

[52] Davis, Ferrell. 4D Ranch , home of Lone Star Boer Goats, Utopia, Texas. From website www.4dranch.com.

[53] Inman, Wanda from Gardnerville, Nevada.

[54] Acevedo, Nora and Edmundo Martinez, Wayne Hanselka, Joe Paschal. "South Texas Cabrito Recipes." Texas Agricultural Extension Service.

NOTES: